# To scare straight or educate? The British experience of day visits to prison for young people

by
Charles Lloyd

**A Research and Planning Unit Report**

Home Office
Research and
Statistics
Department

London: Home Office

# Home Office Research Studies

The Home Office Research Studies are reports on research undertaken by or on behalf of the Home Office. They cover the range of subjects for which the Home Secretary has responsibility. Titles in the series are listed at the back of this report (copies are available from the address on the back cover). Other publications produced by the Research and Planning Unit include Research Findings (which are summaries of research projects), the Research Bulletin (published twice each year) and the annual Research Programme.

## The Research and Statistics Department

The Department consists of the Research and Planning Unit, three Statistics Divisions, the Programme Development Unit and the Economics Unit.

 The Research and Statistics Department is an integral part of the Home Office, serving the Ministers and the department itself, its services, Parliament and the public through research, development and statistics. Information and knowledge from these sources informs policy development and the management of programmes; their dissemination improves wider public understanding of matters of Home Office concern.

*First published 1995*

*Application for reproduction should be made to the Information Section, Research and Planning Unit, Home Office, 50 Queen Anne's Gate, London SW1H 9AT.*

# Foreword

While there is quite a long history of experiments with day visit programmes in the US, their appearance in this country has been comparatively recent and slow to catch on. However, the last four years has seen a progressive rise in the number of such projects from the opening of the first scheme at HMP Garth in 1991 to the twelve operating and nine in planning at the end of 1994. This report is the first published study of British day visit projects and has concentrated on case-studies of three of these schemes. The research has included a literature review of published studies, observation of the schemes in operation and discussions and interviews with samples of inmates, referrers and young people attending the schemes. Conclusions drawn include the observation that while there is no convincing evidence from other research that projects in the US have had an impact on reoffending, there may be a potential for developing day visit projects that aim to educate rather than 'scare straight'.

ROGER TARLING
Head of the Research and Planning Unit

# Acknowledgements

I would like to thank all the young offenders, schoolchildren, inmates, prison staff, probation officers, social workers and teachers who took part in the interviews and discussions. I am also very grateful to Carol Martin who took part in much of the early fieldwork and provided valuable insights and company on those trips. Finally, thanks are also due to George Mair for his comments on drafts of this report.

CHARLES LLOYD

# Contents

# Summary and recommendations

The research consisted of a literature review and case studies of three day visits to prison schemes for young people operating at HMP Garth, Risley and Maidstone. All the projects were observed in operation and discussions and interviews were conducted with samples of inmates, referrers and young people attending the scheme.

## The schemes

### HMP Garth

*A brief description:* young offenders arriving at the prison were searched and escorted to the 'session room'. The presentation consisted of a description of life inside prison: examples of old, stained prison kit, a "piss-pot" and home-made prison weapons used by inmates were shown to the group. Prison was described as a depressing, lonely, isolated, drug-ridden and violent place. The approach of the inmates was confrontational and aggressive: some individuals were shouted and sworn at; more vulnerable members of the group were treated more gently.

- The Garth scheme was based on the original American "scared straight" model and, as a result, was the most confrontational and emotionally charged of the three schemes.

- The confrontational aspect of the scheme was popular with referrers, who regarded it as critical to any impact the scheme might have on reoffending.

- The scheme was mainly targeted at young offenders – although the target group had broadened to include small numbers of young people with no known offending history.

- The project was generally viewed as highly professional.

## HMP Risley

*A **brief description:*** on arrival, the youths were frisked and led through the prison courtyard to the session room in an old wing of the prison. Much of the presentation was similar to that described at Garth, only the inmates were much less confrontational and the atmosphere less intense. A heavy emphasis was put on car crime – and so-called "joy-riding" in particular. They showed explicit photographs and video footage of fatal accidents involving "joy-riders".

- While the Risley scheme had originally been very confrontational, a change in ethos in response to feedback from referrers had led to a more educational approach.

- The project was targeted at motor offenders only – which may have had implications for the referral rate.

- The scheme had a heavy emphasis on the victims of car crime – and the victims of "joy-riding" in particular.

- It consisted of a two-phased approach, with a follow-up session delivered by inmates at probation/social work offices following the prison visit.

## HMP Maidstone

*A **brief description:*** approximately 260 children attended the observed session. They were taken in groups around a prison wing and shown the slopping-out area and a prison cell. They were then taken through the courtyard to the chapel where the presentation took place. The chapel's windows had been blacked-out and drums and musical equipment set up on the rostrum at the front of the chapel. Once the children were seated on the pews, the lights went down and a group of inmates took up the instruments and abruptly broke into a loud rock song with lyrics describing the pain of imprisonment. The children applauded after this – and each subsequent – song. Songs were interspersed with talks about life in prison, including references to powerlessness, depression and suicide. Videos and slides depicting stark images of prisons and prison life were projected on to a large screen behind the inmates.

- The Maidstone scheme represented the least confrontational approach of the three projects.

- The scheme had adopted a very broad target group, including school children not suspected of being involved in crime.

- The observed session was rather chaotic – but the project was at an early stage of development at that time.

## General points

A review of the literature suggests that there is no convincing evidence that schemes in the US have had a significant impact on offending.

The three case studies present three very different approaches to youth crime prevention. The degree of confrontation employed seems to tally with the nature of the target group: with the more confrontational approach of Garth (virtually) reserved for young offenders; the educational approach of Maidstone aimed at school children; and Risley's intensive but broadly educational approach attracting a mixture of offenders and non-offenders.

A number of interviewees pointed out that young people's knowledge of prison was almost entirely based on what they learned from the media – and much of this only served to glamourise prisoners and criminals and depict prisons as holiday camps. Interviews with participants revealed that even if close relatives had served prison sentences, there was often very little discussion of what the experience had been like.

While it is impossible to dismiss entirely some degree of selfish motivation, inmates working on all the schemes appeared to be very enthusiastic and genuinely committed to diverting young people from crime.

Other research has stressed that day visit projects should form an integral part of a larger package of measures designed to prevent offending. There was little evidence of close integration of the visits within court orders or school work: and very little evidence of formalised, one-to-one follow-up sessions with participants.

## Recommendations

- Given the lack of reliable information available to young people on the nature of imprisonment, there seems to be considerable potential for the development of purely educational projects which show school children the reality of life inside British prisons.

- The selection of the target group will have great implications for the nature of the project – confrontational approaches should be restricted to cautioned or convicted offenders.

- Some of the offenders referred to day visit projects were awaiting sentence, their visit constituting part of their pre-sentence assessment by probation officers or social workers. This should be discontinued – particularly in the case of confrontational schemes. The highly negative and threatening portrayal of prison life presented by these projects could lead to self-injury and suicide if offenders receive prison sentences having visited the projects.

- Confrontation should be minimised wherever possible: a minimum of theatrics and a maximum of honesty is likely to ensure that young people are left in no doubt as to the presentation's authenticity.

- Formal assessment procedures should be put in place – particularly for more confrontational schemes. Sensitive and vulnerable young people should be filtered out.

- It is important for referrers to provide inmates in advance with as much information as possible about the young people attending, so that inmates can tailor the presentation to the audience/participants.

- Preparation and follow-up are likely to be critical to any effect of the scheme. Projects for offenders should form an integral part of larger packages of measures designed to prevent offending. It is also important that young offenders get a chance to speak about their visit with their probation officer or social worker on their own, as a formal follow-up procedure.

- While projects seem to be very effectively set up and run by inmates, Governors should keep a close eye on their development and sessions must always be observed by prison staff. Projects should also always be observed by referrers – either *in situ* or on video.

- There are pros and cons to the involvement of long-term prisoners and lifers with these projects. On the one hand, adolescents with little criminal involvement might reject the advice offered because they cannot envisage themselves ever committing very serious crimes and serving long prison sentences. On the other hand, lifers provide continuity, being able to work on projects for long periods of time before being moved, are generally trusted by prison staff and may also contribute to the acceptance of the project amongst other inmates, on account of their prestigious status. They may also have the time and motivation to get schemes running in the first place.

- There is a potential for over-commitment on the part of inmates working on these schemes, which argues for quite careful supervision of the individual inmates involved – perhaps by seconded probation officers or prison psychologists.

- The main forces behind the development of all the case study projects were highly-motivated and charismatic inmates. There was a tendency for projects to go through a crisis when the founding inmates were moved on. Schemes may need considerable support at this stage – with careful selection and "training" of replacement inmates.

- While access to telephones is a problematic issue in prisons, it is imperative that someone associated with the project has access to a telephone to receive referrals. If inmates cannot be allowed such access, it might be possible to have volunteers come in to prisons to handle referrals.

- Projects should build-in the opportunity for feedback from referrers on a regular basis, to inform their development.

# 1 Introduction

In 1978 a local Los Angeles television channel presented a documentary entitled 'Scared Straight', which showed youths attending the 'Juvenile Awareness Project' (JAP) at New Jersey's Rahway State Prison. This documentary was later shown on British television. It showed prisoners lecturing young people in an aggressive and menacing manner about the brutal "realities" of life inside an American prison, including reference to male rape. Since then, the 'Scared Straight' story has conjured up strong emotions both in the US and in the UK. The idea has proved very attractive to many who are frustrated by the apparently intractable problem of juvenile delinquency and in the US, the approach was initially claimed as a panacea for juvenile crime. However, the idea has also proved very unpopular with other sections of the community, who have been concerned about the possible negative consequences of such hostile verbal assaults on vulnerable young people. Recently, a number of projects based to some extent on the 'Scared Straight' approach have started up in this country – the first early in 1991 at HMP Garth. At the end of 1994 there were twelve prisons operating schemes, with nine other prisons planning to set up new projects.

## Methodology

The subject of day visits to prison for young offenders is therefore a very sensitive one – and as a result, quite difficult to research. The researcher was quizzed by a number of interviewees and more informal contacts about the objectivity of his approach in an effort to find out if he had a strong personal agenda. The sensitivity of the subject matter is magnified by the fact that these schemes are based inside prisons, and run by inmates – many of them serving long sentences. For some of the inmates involved, the schemes amounted to much more than a hobby – they were an important part of their lives inside.

The research consisted of a review of the available literature on inmate-run schemes for young offenders and case-studies of three schemes running in this country. The fieldwork, which has been carried out over approximately seven months, has included observation of at least one 'event' at each of the prisons, informal discussions with the inmates and staff involved and formal, semi-structured interviews with representatives of agencies referring young people to the schemes and with samples of the young people themselves.

Due primarily to constraints on time, it has been impossible to collect reconviction data on the participants in the schemes.[1] However, relevant research evidence from the US is briefly reviewed and youths and referrers were asked about the likely impact of the scheme on offending. In order to be meaningful, the collection of reconviction data would have necessitated either random allocation of referrals to projects and control groups or collection of matched data from 'natural' comparison groups. Random allocation in this situation would have been very difficult to implement; and comparison group data would have carried the usual inevitable doubts about whether like had been compared with like. Perhaps more importantly, it would be very difficult to measure the effect of a two- or three-hour visit to a prison in isolation. Any changes in offending behaviour that might take place are likely to be small and might be only realised in combination with other life events. There is also the question of the length of follow-up: would one expect a prison visit to have an immediate impact, a prolonged impact or a delayed impact? It could be argued that the memory of the visit might not have any influence until some time after the event, and considerably further along an offender's criminal career.

## Structure of the report

Chapter Two presents a literature review of the relevant published studies – mostly from the US. The next three chapters present case studies of the three schemes: HMP Garth in Chapter Three, HMP Risley in Chapter Four and HMP Maidstone in Chapter Five. Conclusions are contained in Chapter Six.

---

1    It should be noted that the target groups of two of the schemes studied included young people who had not received any previous convictions.

# 2 A review of the literature

## Introduction

The idea that delinquent juveniles might be persuaded to stop offending by witnessing the predicaments faced by adult prisoners is not a new one in the United States. Brodsky (1970) referred to inmate 'public speaking panels' operating in over twenty states in the 1960s, targeted at religious, educational and youth groups. According to Brodsky, the aims of these programmes were threefold: to try and change the behaviour of teenagers in the audience; to reduce the misinformation and stereotyping surrounding the popular images of prisons and prisoners; and to change the behaviour of inmates, through the personal development of prisoners participating in the schemes. Many of these early schemes such as the Colorado State Penitentiary Inmate Teen Programme (Brodsky 1970) or the San Quentin State Prison 'Squires' programme in California (Finckenauer 1982) involved confrontational, 'aversive' situations. Inmates would describe their criminal careers through delinquency to adult crime and their present life in prison, often with explicit descriptions of the violence and rape they had witnessed while incarcerated. The atmosphere of these discussion groups could become highly charged with emotion and Brodsky reported that young people in the audience were frequently reduced to tears.

However, it was not until the late 1970s that 'youth aversion' or 'juvenile awareness' programmes entered the public domain, after which they proliferated throughout the United States. As with the earlier projects, these programmes were all targeted at juveniles, between the ages of 11 and 17. In 1978 a local Los Angeles television channel presented a documentary entitled 'Scared Straight', which showed youths attending the 'Juvenile Awareness Project' (JAP) at New Jersey's Rahway State Prison. The documentary was later shown on national television. In this film, inmates serving life sentences were shown describing, in unexpurgated detail, the brutal realities of prison life to a group of young people. Descriptions of life in prison, including reference to the inevitability of violence and rape, were made in a menacing, aggressive manner which was intended to scare the young audience. During the film and in accompanying publicity material, the claim was made that 80 to 90 per cent of juveniles attending the JAP were successfully 'scared straight' by their experience. The film was an immediate success, and went on to win an Oscar for the best documentary of the year. The

'Scared Straight' programme was hailed as a successful innovation in tackling juvenile delinquency (Finckenauer 1982).

## Research findings

### Effect on participating youths

Research evaluating the JAP was already underway when the documentary was being made. When the study was published in 1979 (Finckenauer 1979), the findings challenged many of the assumptions made by the documentary. The research attempted to employ an 'experimental' design, whereby a group of 100 juveniles referred to the programme were to be assigned at random to two groups, one of which attended the JAP (the experimental group) and the other which did not (the control group). Unfortunately, completely random allocation of juveniles to the two groups was not achieved due to confusion amongst the agencies referring people to the scheme. Nevertheless, careful checks were made on the two groups to ensure their comparability.

The results showed that while the programme had led to significantly more negative attitudes towards crime amongst the experimental group, those taking part in it also had a significantly higher rate of further offending. While 41 per cent of the experimental group were charged with another offence within six months, only 11 per cent of the controls were so charged. Although there were problems with the design of this study, the more detailed analysis contained in a later report (Finckenauer 1982) presented compelling evidence that the JAP did not prevent subsequent offending.

While a number of other studies have been carried out on the JAP, only one need be mentioned here. Langer (1979) found that over a follow-up period of 22 months, there was a significant tendency for 'control' juveniles to commit more serious offences than programme participants. However, Langer did not even attempt an experimental design and moreover, relied on police and juvenile counsellors to pick out control cases from police files which matched programme participants. This design flaw throws considerable doubt on the study's findings. Despite this, Langer's research gave new hope to the supporters of "scared straight"- style programmes.

While the publication of Finckenauer's negative findings received unusually intense publicity, Langer's contradictory findings and the wave of public support for the scared straight concept ensured that similar programmes sprung up in adult prisons throughout the United States. A number of studies were conducted to assess the success of these schemes in preventing juvenile offending, and three will be described here.

The Juvenile Offenders Learn Truth or JOLT programme, began operation in 1978 at the State Prison of Southern Michigan (Homant and Osowski 1981). Youths participating in the scheme were given a brief tour of the prison and then searched, fingerprinted and put in a cell for several minutes, during which they were given the 'verbal treatment' which consisted of the kind of shouting and taunting that new receptions often experience. They then took part in a confrontational group session akin to the JAP group but with "less earthy language". The JOLT programme was evaluated by the Michigan Department of Corrections in 1979, using an experimental design similar to Finckenauer (Homant and Osowski 1982). The study attempted to compare reoffending rates for 137 JOLT participants with 148 controls. Results showed no significant difference between the two groups in the proportion reoffending after either a three-month or a six-month follow-up period. Again, there were methodological weaknesses with this study (Homant and Osowski 1981). Fifty-eight of the 137 experimental subjects chose not to attend the JOLT session, and were therefore excluded. Then, presumably to maintain approximately equal groups, 59 of the control sample were dropped from the analysis also. However, they were not dropped in a random way – all those excluded were from one particular county. Thus the findings are somewhat weakened. Nevertheless, partly as a result of the publicity surrounding the findings of this study, the scheme was temporarily terminated and then reinstated in a different form. A significant feature of the reinstated project was that there was no verbal intimidation or abuse of the youths by the prisoners.

Another evaluated programme to which reference has already been made is the San Quentin State Prison 'Squires' programme. While broadly similar to the JOLT and JAP programmes, the Squires programme was different in two respects: first, each youth was assigned a 'Squire' or adult inmate who paid particular attention to him during the programme and second, considerable emphasis was put on getting youths to discuss their offences and their background. Again, evaluation of the project took the form of a randomised experiment with 53 males in the experimental group and 55 males in the control group (Lewis 1983). The groups were found to be comparable on a number of measures, although the experimental group was significantly older on average than controls. The two groups were subjected to a battery of attitudinal tests, and arrests and charges were followed-up for a 12-month period. Results showed that the experimental group had significantly less delinquent attitudes towards the police, crime and prison when compared to controls. With regard to reoffending, 81 per cent of the youths who attended the 'Squires' programme were arrested within 12 months, compared with 67 per cent of the control group, although this difference was not statistically significant. The number and nature of charges were very similar for the two groups, but in looking at the time to first arrest, experimentals survived significantly longer before being arrested than controls.

While this might look like a definite positive effect of a scared straight approach on delinquent behaviour, it should be pointed out that this difference might be related to the fact that the experimental group was significantly older than the control group. Further, more complex analysis revealed the suggestion that different subgroups of youths might be responding to the programme in different ways. A rather tentative conclusion was drawn that moderately delinquent youths might profit most from the programme, but that the programme might be detrimental to higher risk youths.

The last of the studies to be described here which focuses on the effect of day visit programmes on juveniles is Buckner and Chesney-Lind's study of the 'Stay Straight Programme' in Oahu, Hawaii. This programme differed from previously described schemes in that it did not involve scare tactics or intimidation. Inmates merely described their experiences and gave advice to the youths. This approach seems to have been a reaction to the criticism surrounding the use of scare tactics in the JAP (e.g. Corrigan 1979). The study focused on 100 males and 50 females who had been referred to the project. A matched sample was then drawn up from police files, picking cases that were similar with regard to age, sex, ethnicity and criminal record. Results showed a significantly higher number of arrests for males who took part in the project over a follow-up period of a year. However, the authors found that part of this negative effect was due to the influence of a subgroup of the 100 males referred to the project, who were also attending a long-term delinquency prevention programme. It was suggested that this subgroup might have met other offenders through the long-term programme and that a "school of crime" effect had occurred, leading to a higher rate of offending for this subgroup.

In conclusion on these studies, there is no convincing evidence presented to show that a scared straight-style project can reduce juvenile delinquent behaviour. If there are any grounds for optimism, they may lie in the indication of a differential impact of the Hawaiin Stay Straight Programme on different subgroups of delinquents (Buckner and Chesney-Lind 1983). This suggestion certainly requires further research. There is also some evidence to suggest that these schemes can have an effect on participants' attitudes towards crime, although given the failure to impact delinquent behaviour, these attitudinal effects may only be temporary. Because of these generally negative findings and concern surrounding the possibility that treating youths in this way might be causing them psychological damage (Finckenauer 1979; O'Malley et al 1993), many of those responsible for running these schemes have either sought to change the nature of their programmes (as in the case of JOLT) or have sought other justifications for their continuance. One beneficial effect claimed by scared-straight supporters is that inmates profit from their involvement and that the prison regime as a whole may also benefit.

### Effect on participating inmates

One of the few studies addressing the question of how participation in day visit programmes affects the inmates involved was carried out on the 'Shape-up' programme at the Colorado State Penitentiary (Keller 1986). The project is described as "a typical post-Scared Straight juvenile awareness programme, in that it rejects the intimidation and scare tactics of Scared Straight." Keller interviewed 15 Shape-up inmates and spent some time involved in participant-observation of the programme. Findings showed that inmates had improved their self-esteem, picked up new skills and had profited personally from being part of a group of inmates, rather than feeling alone and isolated. Keller also referred to the "internalization of law-abiding norms and values": that is, Keller thought that the need for inmates to preach to youths concerning the need to obey the law had affected their own attitudes and opinions. However, there were no attitude questionnaires and no reliable recidivism figures to support his contentions.

Berg (1986) in his evaluation of the Youth Assistance Programme (YAP) in Florida, also focused on the effect of the scheme on inmates. The inmates participating in YAP were trained in a variety of "socio-, and psychodramatic techniques", involving individual and group role-playing. The inmates set up the programme in part as a reaction to the Rahway JAP, rejecting the idea that scaring youths would stop their delinquency. While the study of the programme's impact on the inmates was only part of the overall evaluation, responses to a brief questionnaire given to 20 inmates showed that most inmates seemed to have taken part in the scheme for altruistic reasons. When asked how they had changed since becoming involved in the project, all indicated some sort of increase in self-awareness or self-improvement. Again the nature of this research is qualitative and anecdotal, with no attempt to look at recidivism rates amongst inmates participating in the scheme.

Thus, although there is no convincing evidence to suggest that inmates' recidivism rates are affected by participation in these programmes, the two studies outlined above indicate that they develop personally from their involvement. There would seem little reason to doubt that many long-term prisoners would enjoy and profit personally from contact with young people from outside prison.

## Conclusions

The American experience of scared-straight and similar programmes suggests that such schemes do not have a significant short-term impact on delinquency. None of the studies reviewed here demonstrated a convincing, positive effect of such a programme on offending behaviour. In the absence of positive results, proponents of day visit programmes have dropped the aggressive, confrontational approach of the JAP and have focused on the beneficial effect on inmates and institutions. However, in the last analysis, the survival of non-confrontational day visit programmes in the United States probably relies on the fact that they cost state corrections departments virtually nothing to run.

While the ultimate test of a 'scared straight' project has to be its effect on recidivism, research has found a positive effect of such schemes on attitudes to crime. While these attitudinal changes do not seem to have been automatically translated into changes in offending behaviour, they may provide a basis for further preventative work. Thus a visit to an adult prison might be included as part of a community order, and any reaction to the experience built upon in subsequent parts of the order.

Finally, the American experience with the JAP programme suggests that such projects should be educational rather than confrontational. There is no evidence to suggest that aversive programmes are any more effective than less confrontational ones – and in the absence of such evidence, it has proved hard to maintain confrontational programmes which may cause emotional/psychological trauma for youths attending them. Furthermore, confrontational programmes run the risk of legal action against them for assault or child abuse.

# 3 The Garth Prison Inmate Encounter Scheme

## Background

The Garth scheme is the longest-running and most publicised project in the country. In common with many other inmate-run programmes, the impetus behind the development of the Garth Prison Inmate Encounter Scheme (GPIES) came from a highly motivated and charismatic prisoner serving a long-term sentence at the category B prison. His idea of setting up an encounter group at Garth came originally from the American 'Scared Straight' documentary. Despite some initial resistance to the idea from prison staff, this inmate developed his idea and approached the Governor in early 1990, with a plan to set up a scheme in Garth. Home Office approval was obtained and the first session took place on 17 January 1991. This session was filmed by the BBC, resulting in a documentary "Short, Sharp and Shocking".

As is often the case with new projects, its early operation was not entirely smooth. There were peaks and troughs in its referral rate corresponding with various difficulties and changes in approach. Eight programmes were held over the first six months of the scheme's operation, the referrals consisting mostly of young offenders from a local probation service. The high number of referrals from probation was largely due to the efforts of the prison probation department, which was quite closely involved with the scheme in its early stages. However, due to a breakdown of relations amongst those involved in the scheme, the project went into some decline after the first six months, and referrals ceased to be received from the probation service.

The project was revived towards the end of 1991, but again came into troubled times during the summer of 1992. A research project conducted by a prison psychologist required the random allocation of referrals to a research group and a control group. According to the inmates and staff working on the scheme, this led to some confusion and frustration on the part of referring agencies, who did not entirely understand the reasons for the random allocation and found it frustrating not to be able to refer offenders to the scheme who they thought would benefit from it. This appears to have led to a second steep decline in referrals and the effective closure of the project for four months.

In the autumn of 1992, the project started to receive referrals again. A conscious effort was made to lessen the dependence of the scheme on probation referrals and participants were sought from other agencies. This change was successfully implemented, so that while 75 per cent of referrals prior to October 1992 were from probation services, this figure dropped to 35 per cent from October 1992 to the time of writing (records were not available for the whole of this period). Of the new agencies referring cases to the scheme, two of the most prolific were an employment training centre and the youth court services department of a social services department. The participation of the employment training centre marked a move away from dealing solely with recognised offenders. Although a referrer from this centre felt that most of the young people he had referred were involved in offending behaviour or were about to be, he could not be sure.

Over the period October 1992 to February 1993, the founding inmate was preparing for parole and gradually handed the reins over to other inmates. The project is now run primarily by two inmates serving life sentences. But there is also considerable input from five other inmates, six prison officers and the chaplain.

## Location, target group and referral process

The chaplain took an active interest in the scheme from its start and it has always been based in the chapel complex. One of the rooms serves as an office for the scheme and a telephone line and computer have been provided for the project, to allow the inmates to organise the referrals.

The main target group for the project has been young males aged between 14 and 22. While overall the largest proportion of referrals have come from local probation services, the shift away from probation referrals has led to a drop in the average age of those attending the scheme. While the large majority of participants have been convicted offenders, the greater diversity of referring agencies has led to the attendance of young people who have no recorded criminal history.

Potential referrers can gain an introduction to the scheme either by observing one of the actual sessions or by attending an introductory briefing prepared by the inmates and staff involved. The introductory talk involves a presentation with overheads and a video recording of one of the sessions. Referrals can be made by telephone direct to one of the inmates, who records relevant information on a computerised database and allocates the referral to the next available session.

There were an average of eight young people per group over the period of time that monitoring has been carried out.

## Objectives

The main objectives of the project, as described in the two editions of the 'information package' have changed very little. The original catch-phrase that the founding inmate attached to the project, "Telling the Truth to Youth", seems to have been dropped, but this remains the project's central ethos. Essentially, the GPIES aims to divert young people from further offending behaviour by giving a graphic account of the physical conditions in prison and the personal experience of imprisonment. As with other encounter schemes, an emphasis is put on the fact that inmates were once in the same situation as the young offenders, with the hope that they will be less dismissive of what they have to say than they would a probation officer or a social worker.

A distinguishing feature of the GPIES in comparison to other programmes in England is that the presentation is confrontational: the more recent information package refers to "a psychologically challenging...representation of the environment they may one day find themselves in" and warns that "the team will deliberately instil a sense of anxiety into the youths upon entry into the session room", although "no physical contact will ever take place and a member of staff will remain in the room at all times." The aggressive, energetic nature of the presentation presumably has its roots in the original JAP programme.

The information package is rather unclear on the scheme's target group. While an objective is to "integrate [the programme] into the field of 'intermediate treatment' as an alternative to custody" and the target group is initially described as "persistent young offenders at risk of eventual adult custodial sentence", this section goes on: "or indeed any persons who it is felt might benefit from attending a session." This ambiguity may reflect the changes in targeting policy and the need to keep referral criteria open in order to ensure sufficient numbers.

## A description of the programme

On arrival at the prison, participants tended to be in high spirits: when the group that was observed arriving at the prison was shown into the prison waiting room, they were smoking, drinking soft drinks, joking and jostling each other. When the complete group had assembled, one of the prison officers associated with the scheme walked in, told them to stand up, take their hands out of their pockets and answer to their names as he called them out. They were told to put out their cigarettes and finish their drinks. There was some reluctance to obey these orders: "but I haven't finished my ciggy yet..." and some embarrassed laughter. It was quite difficult for this single prison officer to enforce any discipline. Having checked that everyone was present, the group was taken through the high security double doors, along a corridor into the reception area, where they were made to stand in the middle of the room, side by side, with their toes behind a line painted on the floor. Two other prison officers had joined the original officer and the group began to look more uncomfortable. Their names were read out again and each was told to put any valuables in a locker and was then taken next door to be searched. The search was very thorough. One of the youths had a sweatshirt on with an obscene logo – he was told to take this off and leave it off. When he asked why, the officer replied "prison discipline". Throughout this procedure the youths were ordered around a lot – continually told to take their hands out of their pockets, stop laughing/chatting and stand straight. Although one of the youths kept up some semblance of defiance during this process, the rest looked quite shocked and uncomfortable.

The youths were then escorted though prison corridors and into the "session room", which lies off a corridor to the rear of the chapel. A video camera was set up in this room, which relayed the session live to a television screen in the main chapel itself. People who had brought youths to the prison could therefore watch the encounter scheme in action, along with potential referrers and others interested in the scheme. The participants were told that the session was being recorded, but were not told that their probation/supervision officers were watching the proceedings next door.

On arrival at the session room, the youths were told where to sit (the inmates had a seating plan so that they knew who was who). The prison officer then told them that the inmates were going to be coming in soon, and that they were going to watch a video in the meantime. He then put a video of an episode of the 'Porridge' series on and sat down at the back of the room. After five minutes, the four or five inmates giving the presentation suddenly walked into the session room, dressed in prison overalls. There was an almost audible intake of breath amongst the groups of youths and they were immediately transfixed. The first inmate switched the video off and told the group that they were in Garth to learn what prison life was really like – nothing like Porridge. He then described some "ground rules". "First, we don't want any questions – you're not here to ask questions, you're here to answer them." Second, he told them to give the inmates "a bit of respect – listen to us, watch us and don't take the piss". Finally, he said "we're not here to tell you not to offend – that's what we've all done – we're telling you where you're going to end up."

The approach taken by the first inmate was purposefully hectoring and censorious - youths were told to sit up straight, face the front and listen. At one stage, each participant was told to stand up and say what they were there for. If they replied (as a number did) "I'm here to visit the prison", the inmate shouted that they were serving their first prison sentence – not just visiting. They were then asked what they had been in trouble for. The overall tone of the first quarter of an hour was very much that of a sergeant major bullying a line of troops.

Another inmate then took over and showed the group a video of the reception procedure. The youths were then shown the standard prison kit (which none of the inmates involved with the project normally wear except for work or the presentation). Shirts, trousers, underpants and sheets were passed around for the youths to see and feel – they were old, stained and made of coarse material. When handing around an old pair of underpants, the inmate said "you don't know who's had them before you – it could be someone with AIDS or VD." They were then told about slopping out and shown a fairly old and stained pot. This was put right under their noses and the youths shied away and made faces. The inmate said that while they had their own toilets in Garth, where they were most likely to go (i.e. local prisons) they would have to use a piss-pot in a crowded cell: "when you use it you'll have to do it in front of two other inmates – have to take your trousers and pants off. Imagine what it's like" (the inmate sat on the pot in front of the group). "What do I look like? Imagine the smell of shit..."

The first inmate then introduced himself, beginning "I'm going to tell you who I am now, just in case you think I'm an actor or whatever. I'm not saying 'look up to me', because I'm shite – I'm the fucking lowest of the low." He then passed around a photograph of himself published in a True Crimes magazine and explained that he was a contract killer. "Even 'though I've done this terrible thing, I'm top of the tree here - I get respect." The second inmate then introduced himself – he had been put into care as a child and had been through endless children's homes. He was disruptive and had been sent to approved school, Detention Centres, Young Offender Institutions, prison: "I'm no fucking actor either - I've done 11 years and I'm a killer too. You think you've got it hard – you've got it easy. You say you have to live on £20 or £30 a week. I'd rather live on nothing outside than live in here."

A third inmate did a presentation on prison violence: "around this prison there are walls. Outside these walls there are rules, inside there are no rules. It's bedlam, madness in here – terrible things happen in here." At one stage in his talk he produced a large, PP9 battery wrapped in a sock, which he brought down with a slam on a table. The youths started. The inmate went on to describe how this was used to cosh people in prison. Other weapons were described or shown to the youths and a picture was passed around of a badly-scarred inmate who had been attacked with boiling, sugared water.

The inmate commented: "to survive in here it takes a special kind of person: you have to be a fucking animal."

Other topics covered included suicide and the loneliness of prison life: losing contact with loved ones on the outside and Dear John letters; prison food and tea ("diesel"), which the participants were invited to taste; and the effects of crime on victims. Youths were also told about the possibility of their being raped in prison: "Look at you. You think you're big men don't you? But what are you – 15 or 16? There are a lot of really hard men in here – they see someone young and small like you and that can be enough – they'd do you. These big strong men – they can rape you". Another topic covered in some detail was drug use and the prevalence of drug addiction in prison. An inmate who was serving a sentence for drug offences talked about drug use, dealing, and the inevitability of being caught and imprisoned. He described how some inmates had been forcibly injected with drugs by others.

Throughout the observed presentation if individuals were thought to have stopped attending they were targeted for special treatment – at one stage an inmate went up close to one of the youths, "eye-balled" him, and called him a "stupid little git". Later on, the inmate who was serving a life sentence for a contract killing pretended to lose his temper with one of the youths who he felt was being disruptive. He shouted at the youth "I don't want to be wound up. I'm a killer not a fucking probation officer." This inmate then said that if he did not leave the room he would lose control – and walked out. He came straight into the chapel where the observers were watching the session and was relaxed, smiling and in complete control. On another occasion, one of the inmates shouted at one of the youths: "don't look at the wall – look at me. If I see you in here I'll get you, I've got nothing to lose. Don't think you can take me for a cunt and don't look at me with that arrogant expression. Inside here they'd do you for just looking like that."

However, it was noticeable during the presentations that inmates were careful not to bully the more vulnerable-seeming members of the group. One boy who had been referred from a regional secure unit seemed quiet and sensitive and he was given very sympathetic treatment. Another youth was known to have difficulty controlling his anger and he too was given much softer treatment.

The whole session took between two and three hours. At the end of the presentation the first inmate said "we're off now – in an hour we'll be banged up in our cells. Make sure you always go back to your home – not a cell." The inmates then walked out. When they left the room the youths visibly breathed a sigh of relief. The prison officer then tried to sum up, but the youths were too relieved and excited to listen. They were then escorted out of the prison.

# Views of referrers

## The agencies

Staff at three of the principal agencies referring youths to the GPIES were interviewed: all three agencies had referred around 40 offenders to the scheme. The first of these agencies was a probation centre that provided group work and supervision for probation orders with 1A3 requirements (Criminal Justice Act 1991). Staff at this centre used the Garth project as one of forty three-hour components that made up the 1A3 order. However, the visit was not specifically referred to in court and was not therefore a formal requirement. The probation officer interviewed had used the project on an occasional basis since its inception and had sent at least five groups to the prison, consisting of between seven and eight offenders on each occasion. The second referring agency was a job training/assessment centre for 16-to 18-year-olds, dealing with young people referred mostly by career services but also by special schools. The young people referred from the job training agency were therefore very different from those referred from the probation centre: while many bragged about their criminal behaviour, the two staff interviewed suspected that some of this was bravado: many of them were "street-wise but incredibly naive". The staff referred the "particularly trouble-some" youths to the GPIES – and suspected that the majority had been involved in some kind of offending behaviour. The third agency was a specialist youth court services team, consisting of 16 social workers and four probation officers working on the same site. Most of these staff were case workers, but three of the social workers constituted the "programme team", responsible for developing and running programmes – the views of this team were sought in a group interview. The specialist team was similar to the probation centre, in that they were responsible for developing and running specialist programmes for high tariff supervision orders. The GPIES repre-sented one of these programmes. The team also used a scheme running at HMP Nottingham. Social services referrals to the GPIES were younger than the probation centre referrals, falling into the 13- to 17-year-age group; only one had attended at the pre-sentence stage – the rest were on supervision orders with requirements. Attendance at Garth was included in Programme Reports presented to the courts as part of the social services recommenda-tion.

## Type of referrals

All referrers were asked how they selected offenders for referral to GPIES. The probation centre excluded offenders with previous adult prison sentences, those who were too emotionally volatile and anyone outside the 17 to 30 age range. In certain cases, they had taken youths who were quite unstable, but had warned the inmates beforehand and they had "gone easy on them". The staff made the point that it was imperative to give inmates sufficient information on referrals before they attended, to allow inmates to target their approach to individuals in the group. While attendance was ultimately voluntary, those offenders who satisfied the criteria for attendance were referred to the project – any objections would be listened to, but usually overcome. Around 80 per cent of all offenders attending the probation centre went to Garth as part of their orders.

The training centre did not force people to attend the scheme – many were not even approached, but volunteered, on hearing about the scheme from friends. All potential referrals were warned that they would be subjected to a long and potentially threatening presentation delivered by murderers and violent offenders. Some potential referrals decided that they did not want to attend – others wanted to but were not allowed, due to their emotional vulnerability or because they were at serious risk of receiving an adult custodial sentence. The latter group were barred on the basis that, should they receive an adult prison sentence or find themselves remanded in custody with such a sentence in prospect, the highly negative picture painted by the Garth project could remain in their minds and they might be more likely to attempt suicide because of their exaggerated fear of the starkness and brutality of prison life. A member of staff described this as an "ethical problem with the Garth scheme...just one diversion from a life of crime could be considered a considerable success – but one suicide would be a complete disaster." This project worker had talked to the GPIES inmates about this issue and they had expressed an interest in providing a counselling service for young offenders facing custody, with the message that, in reality, nearly everyone survived imprisonment relatively unscathed. However, this issue remained a considerable problem for this project worker.

The third agency, the social services programme team, only referred offenders on supervision orders with requirements to the project. The team did not filter out many people on the grounds of emotional vulnerability. Only the most serious, recidivist offenders were referred to Garth, lower tariff offenders were referred to a scheme at HMP Nottingham, which adopted a less confrontational approach. Programme team staff found it very useful to be able to have two different types of projects to refer to. None of the offenders had actually refused to attend – but staff made it sound like a compulsory requirement, so offenders thought they had no choice in any case. However, they had found that approximately a quarter of the offenders originally referred to the GPIES did not actually attend. This was due to offenders getting prison sentences, absconding or later being considered inappropriate.

## Overall impression

With regard to their overall impression of the GPIES, all referrers were very positive: they thought the project was very well run: "professional" was a word used frequently by the majority of interviewees. While some reference was made to the earlier problems with the referral process during the random allocation research, the present referral system was universally described as efficient. Relations with inmates running the scheme were described as very good: close working relationships had been struck up, so that referrers felt they could give feedback to the inmates and their advice would be taken on board. The targeting of individuals in the groups on the basis of information received by referrers was commended by several interviewees – and contributed to the "professional" image of the scheme.

## Level of confrontation

All interviewees thought that the exhausting, stressful, confrontational nature of the GPIES was a major strength. One of the probation officers interviewed at the probation centre described his clients as needing "firm boundaries" and the inmates as "firm but fair". Offenders tended to strut in to the prison, with their chests stuck out, thinking to themselves "they're not gonna scare me", but by the end of the session they were quite subdued. The officer summed up this process as "in like a lion, out like a lamb", and viewed it as critical to any impact of the project. He did not think offenders should be allowed to ask questions, for fear of the inmates getting too "pally-pally" with the offenders. He described how the inmates had recently started lining up outside the encounter room, as the participants left, "eyeballing" them and not responding when the youths said goodbye or thanked them. He thought this was very effective and fitted well with the scheme's aims. The training centre staff stated that their referrals were not at all put-out by the confrontation – they knew they would walk out of the prison untouched. They thought that those who "got picked on" were so for a reason: one of the interviewees said he had "never seen anyone who couldn't hack it put in that situation." Without the confrontation, the training centre staff could not see the scheme having any effect. The youth court staff were similarly positive about the confrontational aspects of the GPIES: in their view the confrontational aspect was its great strength. One of the staff thought there could be a bit more confrontation; one thought it was about right and the other, while she had some qualms about seeing some of the kids being made to sit on a piss-pot, would not change the project in this respect.

## Criticisms

While referrers' overall assessments of the GPIES were universally very favourable, all made some criticisms or suggestions for change. Referrers from two of the agencies thought that the presentation was too long, although the youth court services staff thought the length of the presentation was perfect: "short enough to maintain interest, long enough to be exhausting." Other issues raised under the question of how referrers would improve the GPIES included abandoning the prison officer component after the presentation (which none of the referrers thought was effective) and injecting a "bit more street cred" into the scheme. It was felt by one of the referrers that some of the lifers were "a bit out of touch" – a few more short-term prisoners would be an improvement. A number of referrers also regretted the apparent abandonment of the highly emotional component carried out by one of inmates. [The researcher has viewed video footage of this component, during which the inmate, who was himself moved to tears, described how he missed his daughter.]

## Follow-up

On the issue of follow-up, both the probation officers and social workers referred to de-briefing offenders in the encounter room after the presentation. All felt this was very important – as offenders could be quite distraught and/or excitable. All referrers encouraged offenders to write to the inmates as a follow-up exercise – and this formed part of the literacy training provided by the training centre. The youth court team had to journey some distance to the project, and staff referred to further de-briefing in the van on the way home. The visit was then followed by a group session, where they discussed their visit and watched the BBC documentary on the project. However, it was pointed out, while the staff would have been eager to do so, there was simply not enough time to follow up the visit with individual sessions to allow offenders to voice their private opinions and feelings concerning their experience.

## Colleagues' views

Referrers were asked what colleagues thought of the scheme. While probation staff generally accepted the scheme, the probation centre staff said there were one or two who had reservations. These were always the officers who had not visited the project: once doubters went to see the GPIES in action, they came away impressed. No supervising officer holding offenders' probation orders had ever refused to allow his client to visit Garth. However, it was pointed out that the project had lost a lot of friends over the random allocation episode. There had been some debate amongst social services colleagues of the youth court team about whether the GPIES was "morally OK". Some staff had mixed feelings but, again, it was thought that once staff actually visited the scheme, any fears were laid to rest.

## Effectiveness

Finally, on the question of effectiveness, responses were understandably qualified and indirect. A probation officer pointed out that "there would never be a miracle cure [for offending]...being, realistic, there would only be a long-term effect in a few cases." He went on to describe the issue of effectiveness as very complex: the Garth visit was only one part of a whole package of work – so it was impossible to address the question of what effect it had on its own. This said, the officer thought that the GPIES did bring home the unpleasant nature of prison life and that in some cases this became ingrained on young offenders minds for a long time. One of the training centre staff suggested that the project had little effect on the "gobby" participants and more on the quieter ones. He thought that for most referrals there was a high initial impact for two to three weeks, at the maximum. Thereafter, in most cases, there were just selective memories and if they went out with their mates at that point, they would most likely commit offences if the others did. However, with some individuals there seemed to be a strong and lasting effect – some seemed to say "that's it – I'm not offending again." The court services team thought that the impact of the GPIES might not be realised for many years. "This type of approach can lay a seed in an offender's conscience that might not bear fruit for some time." They too thought it was very difficult to separate the effect of the project from the other things that were going on in offenders' lives: other work on their supervision orders; relationship and employment changes etc. However the team was in no doubt that the visit affected attitudes to imprisonment – offenders were always saying that they had been shocked to find out various things that the prisoners had told them. They also always remembered the visit – if there was any part of their supervision orders they could recall, it was the visit to Garth.

## Views of participants

Six young offenders were interviewed, all male: two who had attended the probation centre and four who were referred from the youth court services team. The probation referrals were interviewed in an office in the probation centre and the social services referrals were interviewed in an office in the youth court team building. The probation referrals were interviewed some time after their attendance – one had attended a year before interview; the other two years before – and were aged 24 and 25 respectively. The social services referrals had attended GPIES two weeks before their interviews and were aged between 14 and 17.

## Criminal history

Interviewees were first asked about their criminal histories. The two probationers had a number of previous convictions; one had been convicted of fraud and deception offences and had spent two weeks on remand at Wormwood Scrubs before receiving his present order. The other had a number of previous convictions for TWOC and had been in a Detention Centre; a Young Offender Institution and adult prisons (but, as he stressed, only Category C or open prisons). Only one of the offenders on supervision orders had no previous convictions (and he had been cautioned); the other three had all been previously convicted of burglary offences – amongst others. Only one had been imprisoned – he had spent a week on remand in Glen Parva. Offenders had mostly received their current orders for multiple offences – in many cases including burglary offences.

## Knowledge of prison system

It was thought important to ask offenders about their knowledge of the prison system prior to their visit to Garth, in order to try to gauge whether the scheme had any impact in terms of creating an image or impression of imprisonment. As has been mentioned, one offender had already had considerable first-hand experience of imprisonment and two others had spent short periods on remand. Of the others (all social services), one said that he had not known much about prison before he went to Garth – although his brother had been inside for two years, they had not really discussed it. Another's father had been "in and out of prison, serving 18-month sentences until he died seven years ago". This offender had visited his father inside, but he had been young and remembered little. The other knew friends who had "been inside", but they had not talked about it.

## Views on the scheme

All the offenders, including those who had attended one or two years previously, could remember their visits clearly and produced accurate and quite detailed accounts of the programme without prompting. Most had been scared – or at least admitted reluctantly to having been made to feel nervous – by the size, manner and criminal records of the inmates: one offender referred to "a six foot nutter"; another said "I'd like to say they didn't [frighten me], but they did!". Only one offender said they had not frightened him, and that the shouting and aggression had been "a waste of time", but the researcher was left with the impression that this could have been a case of macho bravado. While frightened, the offenders also seemed to regard the inmates with a mixture of awe, pity and gratitude for trying to do something on their behalf.

Offenders also spoke of the "intense" atmosphere: one described how "the session was non-stop – they zeroed in on you – and you couldn't relax for a second." Accounts of prison violence (particularly the slamming down of the PP9 battery on the table), homosexuality, prison clothes and prison food stuck in most of the offenders' memories. However, the offender who had been inside for some time thought the inmates had "beefed it up a bit" – he had heard of homosexuality and rape going on, but he did not think it was nearly as common as they had made out. There were other signs that those with previous custodial experience were more sceptical than the others – they were obviously less shocked by the appearance of prison clothes, piss-pots and food; and the descriptions of overcrowded and unpleasant cells.

Attitudes towards the prison officers were, perhaps unsurprisingly, negative: the offenders generally disliked and resented being ordered around by them. One offender said "even my Mum doesn't order me about like that"; another described them as "wankers – they didn't do fuck all..." One offender had found the way inmates had ordered them around "as if they were in control of everything" hypocritical: as he pointed out, "they weren't [in control], they were inside Garth for a start." This offender had wanted to ask some questions, and had been frustrated by the inmates' refusal to allow him to.

## Effectiveness

With regard to the effect the visit had had on them, the offenders were generally positive. One of the probationers said that the GPIES visit and the probation order had kept him out of trouble for two years. The thought of Garth prison had been at the back of his mind since he went there – and he would never forget it. However, he also said that he had started a family and this had helped him to settle down. The other probationer thought the scheme had "definitely had an effect" on him – he said it "definitely made me less likely to offend" and was "one of the main factors" that had made him decide to stop offending: one big sentence and he could end up some-where like Garth. However, again there were other causes: his wife was pregnant and this had given him "a good kick up the arse".

The offenders on supervision orders tended to explain the impact of the scheme in terms of strengthening their resolve to stop offending: one said the visit had "completely stopped me offending – before I'd only slightly made the decision – after the trip I was definite". Another said GPIES had only contributed "a bit" to his resolve to stay out of prison – a week on remand in Glen Parva and getting a job and a girlfriend had been more important. Several expressed the view that they were too young to be imprisoned in any case, and one thought he might well commit further offences while he was still only 14. The prospect of a long-term prison sentence at Garth seemed a very long way off for the youngest offenders.

## Discussion

Perhaps the salient feature of the GPIES is the intense nature of the presentation. The fully-observed session was confrontational: many of the youths were shouted at and intimidated. Inmates described this aggressive approach as being necessary to "get through to" the youths. They felt they could not afford to lose the attention of any of the participants – and were wary of trouble-makers who might disrupt the group by asking questions out of turn or trying to make the others laugh. As a result the atmosphere of the observed group was that of a strictly-governed classroom in the days when children were not encouraged to ask any questions. Indeed one of the brighter of the participants asked a number of perfectly reasonable questions, which got replies like "you're not in school now you know" and "did I say I wanted questions?". The inmates' approach seems to stem from a preoccupation with the danger of losing control of the group. Apparently this has occasionally happened to some extent with the GPIES. I was told of one particular inmate who had tried to give a presentation, but had been "too weak" – and had lost the attention of the group. Presumably therefore, there is some basis for this preoccupation, but in the observed session, the level of confrontation did not seem to be proportional to what misbehaviour there was on the part of the youths.

This said, the confrontational aspect of the scheme was one of its best attributes in the eyes of referrers: without this they thought it would lose any impact it might have on offending. In defence, reference was made to the targeting of the confrontation so that only youths who were thought able to cope with it were subjected to aggression. Some of the youths were clearly very unruly and disruptive and many referrers felt that the "sergeant major" approach was the only way to get the message through to them. One referrer who was not formally interviewed expressed great satisfaction at seeing her very difficult and abusive client sitting bolt upright and listening to every word uttered during the presentation.

GPIES presentations can be intensely emotional. While the fully-observed group consisted of unusually young participants, many of the other groups were composed of offenders in their twenties. With these groups, where a number of the participants had families, more emphasis was put on their responsibility as fathers and how they would miss their family if incarcerated. A video of a previous session with one such group of older participants showed an inmate talking about how he missed his wife and children. He showed the youths a photograph of his daughter and told them he had not spoken to her properly in over six years. He focused in particular on the participants who had children and asked them how they could be so selfish and stupid to throw away the most important things in life: spending time with people you cared for. By the finish, the inmate was tearful and the youths looked very upset.

The dedication of the inmates involved with the project seemed very great. Of course, it is impossible to discount selfish motives. While the possibility of increased eligibility for parole was vigorously denied by the inmates, involvement in the scheme can certainly have done them no harm. Moreover, more positively, the scheme gave inmates a break from a very dull and monotonous life and the chance of contact with people from outside the prison: both youths and referrers. The inmates most intimately involved with the scheme seemed to be completely genuine in their desire to steer young people away from crime. Some of the inmates expressed remorse for the very serious crimes they had committed and working with youths in this way seemed to offer some way of making partial amends.

There did seem to be a more general benefit to the prison in terms of improved relations between prison officers and inmates working on the project, although this would require more detailed study. Some of the prison officers had worked on the project during their leisure time and one expressed her pleasure at being able to do something "positive", rather than locking people up all day. Of course, it should not be assumed that the attitudes expressed by staff and inmates involved in the project extend to the rest. GPIES inmates reported being "wound up" by other inmates about the project and many of the prison officers who did not work on the scheme were reportedly very suspicious of it, presumably because it appeared to give too much power to inmates. However, the researcher did not have time to interview inmates and staff not involved with the scheme. While, for operational reasons, the prison officers' involvement with the scheme may be crucial to its survival – and may contribute in some degree to better relations in the prison – views of referrers and participants were broadly negative. Youths tended to have a knee-jerk reaction to prison officers, bracketing them with police officers as "the enemy".

Another important feature of the Garth project is its professionalism. The presentation to potential referrers and the computerised referral system were impressive. Referrers were impressed by the scheme's professionalism

– in particular the way inmates requested information on participants' characteristics and criminal histories in order to target their presentation. The GPIES' professionalism is no doubt partly due to the fact that it is the longest running of the projects in this country but also seems to be due to the considerable support it has received from the Chaplain and the Governor. Without such support, it would have been impossible to provide inmates with access to a telephone, computer and office. However, the smooth-running and professional nature of the scheme is also a consequence of the bright and dedicated inmates working on it.

An important issue raised in one of the interviews with referrers was that of the potential for the scheme contributing to suicides in prison. Some offenders were sent to Garth at the pre-sentence stage, and inmates sometimes wrote up reports on participants to include in presentations to the court. There is a serious danger that, if offenders are given custodial sentences immediately after attending the scheme, the highly negative and frightening portrayal of prison-life depicted by the GPIES will increase their feelings of desperation. Relevant here are the comments of one of the interviewed youths: "I know I wouldn't survive in one of those prisons. I don't think I would even if I was old enough." The use of the GPIES at the pre-sentence stage seems highly questionable.

In conclusion, the GPIES is a very efficient scheme with a dedicated team of inmates and officers. There seems little question that the project is beneficial to the inmates involved. It is also possible that the scheme contributes to better relations between staff and inmates. Whether or not the scheme has any effect on the offending behaviour of those who attend is another matter; five of the six youths interviewed thought the visit would help them stop offending in the future. However, whether these words bore fruit in terms of actual desistance is, of course, open to question.

# 4 The Risley Car-Related Crime Scheme

## Background

As with the GPIES, the motivating force behind the development of the Risley Car-Related Crime Scheme (CRCS) came from inmates. However, its early development differed from Garth in having a considerable input from the local community. In November 1991 two young children were killed by a car driven by so-called "joy-riders" in Toxteth, Liverpool. The particular street where they were killed, Granby Street, was a notorious location for joy-riding and the local neighbourhood reacted by placing barricades across the roads and forming a pressure group, the Granby Street Mothers.

Two category C inmates then serving sentences for serious motor offences ("ram-raiding") happened to come from this particular part of Toxteth and actually knew one of the bereaved families. They had the idea of setting up a project aimed at diverting Toxteth youths from joy-riding, with the aim of preventing such horrific accidents. With the support of the Governor, the Granby Street Mothers were contacted, along with Merseyside Probation, Merseyside Police and Liverpool Social Services. Links with Merseyside Probation were easily forged, as one of the founding inmates had worked as a sessional worker on a community service scheme in Merseyside. While some initial scepticism was apparently expressed by the police, it was suggested by one interviewee that a pressing motive for their eventual participation lay in the breakdown in communication that had occurred between the police and the local community in Toxteth. A steering group was set up consisting of representatives of the above-mentioned agencies, the Governor, the two inmates, seconded probation staff and prison officers. It was agreed that a pilot project would be set up.

Before the pilot project, the two founding inmates went to Garth to observe the GPIES. As a result, the programme took its basic outline from the Garth project, although it was focused much more heavily on offending behaviour – and car crime in particular. Over the course of the three pilot sessions, attention was focused solely on Toxteth, participants consisting of probationers convicted of motor offences in the Toxteth area. The Risley initiative was therefore originally a local reaction to a local problem.

An important feature of the programme outline was that it had two distinct phases: first, there was the prison-based presentation which broadly followed the format of GPIES; second, there was a follow-up session in the community, whereby inmates went out to the probation office and had a more informal talk with the offenders, during which they were invited to ask questions about the inmates and their experience of imprisonment. This marked a significant departure from the GPIES programme.

The three pilot schemes took place on subsequent months, starting in March 1992. The project was therefore up and running within four months of the joy-riding incident that led to its inception. After the apparent success of the pilots, referrals were sought through the distribution of a letter and a flyer giving a brief summary of the project and its aims to social services and probation offices.

Fourteen sessions took place over the next seven months, with a total of 74 referrals: an average of five per session. There followed a three-month period where no sessions were held at all. Then six sessions were held over a three-month period, but with few participants in each, followed by another three-month lull. Since then, the project has been changed somewhat and an information pack has been produced, referring to a "New Approach." The primary aim of the new approach seems to have been to make the scheme less confrontational and was introduced in response to feedback from referral agencies, whose representatives had found some of the sessions too aggressive. Since the introduction of the new approach in the summer of 1993, there has been a three-month period where the scheme has been operating on a more regular basis.

While every attempt was made to ensure that the second, follow-up phase of each programme took place, this was logistically much more difficult to arrange than the session in prison. After the project had been running for some time, the follow-ups became less frequent. This was apparently due in part to difficulties in providing staff to escort prisoners but may also have been associated with the fact that on occasions, visits were arranged but offenders failed to turn up at the probation/social services offices. With the introduction of the new approach, follow-ups again became a regular and expected part of the programme.

The development of the CRCS has therefore not been completely smooth – its fortunes seem to have waxed and waned somewhat, as one might expect of any new project of its kind. However, as one interviewee pointed out, there have been a number of spurs at critical times which have maintained motivation and interest in the project. According to this respondent, an important motivator early on was the community interest. Then when the scheme was properly under way, there was the excitement induced by the considerable media attention that the project attracted. A final incentive was the prestigious award won by the two prison officers associated with the project for the work they had done on the scheme. To these might be added the "new approach", which has resulted in a new wave of enthusiasm.

## Location, target group and referral process

To begin with, the project had been based in the chapel. The chapel was chosen because the prison chaplain was supportive of the scheme and because it represented one of the few available spaces within the prison. However, when the project had been running for about fifteen months, it was moved to a room in the old reception wing of the prison.

Referrals to the scheme were made through the two prison officers involved: there was no office or telephone manned by inmates. The close involvement of prison staff at Risley is in marked contrast to the GPIES – where they appeared to play a quite peripheral role.

The large majority of the participants were referred by social services in the Liverpool and Manchester areas. But as with the GPIES, there was a widening of the target group over the course of the scheme's operation. More recently, young people were referred from youth clubs and youth projects that did not necessarily deal with convicted offenders. However, the emphasis remained on car crime: referrals were all supposed to be involved in offending of this type.

## Objectives

A main aim of the CRCS is to challenge the view held by many young offenders that joy-riding is a trivial offence, by demonstrating to motor offenders what the consequences of such behaviour can be – both for the victims of the crime and for the offenders themselves. The emphasis on the victims of joy-riding stems from the scheme's original development as a response to the deaths of the two young children in Toxteth. The effect of car crime on the offenders themselves is addressed through showing participants how futile, degrading and dangerous life can be in an adult prison. While many of the objectives therefore coincide with those of the GPIES, the heavy emphasis on victims is a distinctive feature of the CRCS.

## A description of the programme

The observed session was the first that took place after the introduction of the "New Approach". On arrival, the three youths attending the scheme were frisked by one of the officers involved with the project and then led through the prison courtyard to the old reception wing. On the way, a group of inmates passed the youths and staring at them, made loud comments about "the car thieves". Apparently, joy-riders and car thieves are held in very low esteem in the prison and this was completely unrehearsed. Nevertheless, the youths looked very discomforted by the experience.

On reaching the wing, the youths went down a central corridor and were then shown into a small room on the right. Ahead of them as they turned, the corridor was screened off, and behind this screen was a television and some chairs for the youths' social workers and the inmates involved with the scheme. The small room in which the session was to take place contained a hard bench, television screen, video camera and numerous photographs of gruesome car crash scenes affixed to the wall. Once the youths had entered the session room, the television in the corridor was switched on and the session began. Unfortunately, as this was the first session held in the wing there were some problems with the sound system, and it was hard to distinguish some of what was said. The first inmate to go in took the group through a general account of prison life. A video was shown of conditions in the old allocation wing in Risley when it was a remand centre and showed the inmates slopping out (cells at Risley now have toilets). A similar routine to that described in the GPIES was then followed with the prison kit and a pot. The inmates seemed to be well-rehearsed. While inmates "performed" in the session room, other inmates hung around in the corridor, watching the session on the television and waiting for their cue to go in to the session room – their nervousness and concentration very like that of actors waiting to go on stage. This analogy was also brought to mind by the fact that on completing his part in the presentation, the first inmate went into another room of the corridor and changed from his prison overalls (his "costume") into smart, casual clothes.

When an inmate came out of the session room he told the other inmates how the individual participants were responding – and who they should focus their attention on. The youths were also watched carefully on the screen by inmates not currently involved in the presentation, to observe their reactions. One of the youths seemed quite cocky and uninterested – and indeed had done so since his arrival at the prison gate. While particular attention was paid to him, this was in terms of asking him to listen, rather than through the aggressive approach taken at Garth.

After the session on prison conditions, two other inmates delivered the car crime presentation, both of whom had been imprisoned for motor offences. They stressed how many inmates in Risley were serving long sentences for car crime. They then showed a video taken by the police as they chased joy-riders. During one chase a pedestrian was knocked down and in the course of another, a joy-rider on a motorbike crashed, with what looked like fatal consequences. There was also video footage of the Granby Street Mothers and the barricades they set up and of one of the bereaved mothers crying at her child's funeral. Videos were also shown of interviews with two inmates – one of whom had beaten up and seriously injured a man who had killed his child through drink driving and another who had killed someone while driving a stolen car. Lastly, some of the unpleasant photographs of fatal car accidents were passed around to show what could happen as a result of joy-riding.

After the presentation, the youths were taken out to the prison gate, where they met their social workers and left the prison. The whole session took about two hours.

It did not prove possible to observe a follow-up session. However, these were described as less formal and more interactive: youths were encouraged to ask the inmates questions about themselves and life in prison.

## Views of referrers

### The agencies and types of referrals

Interviews were carried out with representatives from three agencies that had referred youths to the CRCS. The first was a motor project, which attracted referrals from the probation service and social services – although other youths heard about the scheme by word of mouth and attended volun-tarily. The youths, aged between 16 and 19 spend most of their time learning about motor vehicle maintenance – a course which ended in a National Vocational Qualification. The "carrot" to hold their interest in the course was a trip to a motocross motorbike track once a week. If the youths did 21 hours work over the week, they got to drive the motorbikes. According to the project worker, nearly all of the youths had previously been involved in car crime and a lot had been joy-riding or at least driving around in stolen cars. This was apparently the norm on the big estates, where youths took it in turns to drive stolen cars that had been brought on to the estate. Kids vied to be "top jockeys" – the top drivers who knew how to handle a car. The project worker had referred at least 60 youths to the CRCS. He referred all the youths at the motor project to Risley, except for non-offenders, those not emotionally able to handle the presentation and some who had previous experience of custody.

The other two agencies were both part of separate inner-city social services departments. One interviewee was a central referring agent for three social service field teams. He had referred 16 offenders involved with car crime to the CRCS and had been in contact with the scheme since its inception. He used the project at the pre-sentence phase, in the preparation of PSRs and as part of supervision packages. Two representatives of the other social services department were interviewed – both were main grade social workers working in a "multi-service centre". The CRCS was used as one component of a high tariff supervision order for 15- to 17-year-olds. The policy was only to use the project as an alternative to custody. As a result, most of the referrals to the project had had a number of previous convictions, or if not, they had been convicted of a serious offence such as aggravated TWOC. Although the interviewees had only referred 16 offenders between them, the project was proving very popular with sentencers in their city.

## Overall impressions and level of confrontation

Referrers were generally positive about the CRCS. The motor project worker found it quite easy to refer people to the project – although one had to fit in with the scheme's timetable. The social workers also found it easy to refer their clients – although one mentioned that it would be useful to have written confirmation that offenders would be allowed to attend.

All interviewees seemed to be aware of the change in the level of confrontation over the course of the scheme's development. However, opinions varied as to the merit of this change. The motor project worker thought the scheme had "lost a bit of its bite...If the lads are cocky and think they're hard, the inmates have to be harder". He was keen on a tough approach, to show them what prison was like. Nevertheless, he did think that there was scope for varying the type of presentation according to the type of group visiting. Some youths did not need a strict approach; others did. By contrast, the two social workers interviewed together were pleased with the less aggressive approach. If inmates were too confrontational and theatrical, it could have a negative effect, especially when offenders saw them on the follow-up visit, when they were friendly and relaxed. Offenders could dismiss the whole presentation on this basis. However, one of the two interviewees felt the prison discipline aspect was important: he approved of the "stop smirking" approach, and did not want the project to get any softer on the offenders. The other social services referrer thought there was only aggression towards the youths in order to "break down the macho posturing" amongst them. The boys had their own "pecking order" and, in his opinion, it was sometimes necessary for the inmates to establish themselves at the top of that order. He had always told his clients that if they could not "handle it", they should just put their hand up. He would see this on the video and come and get them out of there.

## Follow-up

The follow-up sessions were popular with all four referrers. All referred to the atmosphere in these sessions being very different from the prison presentation: as one referrer pointed out, "the kids are on their home ground and ask a lot of questions" – these follow-ups were much more *ad-hoc* and informal. Another of the referrers thought that the follow-up sessions could counter the impression that some youths had that the prison presentation was a theatrical performance and that the inmates had been "bullshitting" them. However, there were some indications that the follow-ups could be hard to arrange on occasions – sometimes they had not taken place. Releasing inmates into the community obviously had its risks and without the Governor's strong support for the scheme, this component of the project would have been impossible. Interestingly, the motor project worker reported that some youths did not attend the follow-up session because they had been frightened by the inmates at the presentation.

Apart from these inmate-led follow-ups there seemed to be very little formal follow-up by the social workers or the project worker. If the youths wanted to talk about it, discussions took place – but as with other projects, there were no formalised one-to-one sessions arranged to discuss the youths' impressions of the scheme.

## Colleagues' views

The two social workers interviewed from one large city social services department thought the scheme was under-used for two main reasons: first, a number of their colleagues' were either suspicious of the scheme and its confrontational nature or were too apathetic to look for new ways to work with offenders; second, it had not been sold enough. The use of the scheme had been practitioner-led, rather than management-led. They were surprised that magistrates had not started asking for visits to Risley as part of supervision orders – and thought this might well happen in the future. If there was no local policy, social workers in court may well know nothing about the scheme and this could prove embarrassing for the Department.

## Effectiveness

One of the social workers and the project worker both expressed the view that the scheme could have little impact in isolation. The social worker thought that on its own, the project's impact "would last about a fortnight": it was only as part of an overall programme that the scheme might have an effect on offending behaviour. If it did have an effect, he thought it was first, because inmates had "street credibility" that social workers and probation officers could never hope to have and second, because it deglamourised crime. Some of the inmates were local "folk heroes" – they had been notorious, big-time criminals and young offenders were in awe of them. A major strength of the scheme was that during the presentation, these so-called "hard men" came across as powerless and depressed "failures".

The other two social workers appeared somewhat divided in their opinions. One expressed the view that he used the scheme solely to "win" orders: magistrates were very keen on the project (in his opinion because it was run by inmates rather than social workers) and a visit to Risley was therefore a powerful component to attach to a supervision order and could be used to divert young people from imprisonment. However, he did not think it had any effect at all: an example was cited of one of the earliest referrals to the scheme – a notorious local thief. At one stage during the session when the inmates' backs were turned, this young offender had stolen a police scanning devise that had formed part of the presentation. After the youths had left, the inmates realised that it was missing and played back the video of the presentation. The youth could be plainly seen picking up the device and putting it in his pocket.

The other social worker was more sanguine about the scheme's effectiveness. He thought the project broke down offenders' excuses for their offending behaviour by making them face up to the impact on victims. Indeed, he thought that if the scheme did have an impact, it was through the photographs of children killed by joy-riders and their bereaved mothers rather than through making the youths scared of imprisonment.

## Views of participants

Unfortunately, due to time constraints and interview cancellations only two participants were interviewed – both of whom were attending the motor project. Both interviewees reported having no previous convictions, but one had been cautioned for a criminal damage offence and openly admitted to having been a passenger in stolen cars and the other had been cautioned for shoplifting, assault on a police officer and a drug offence and had also been a passenger in stolen cars.

Both interviewees had relatives who had "been inside": in one case "some of my uncles" and in the other, his father. However, in neither case had their relatives spoken very much about their experiences and the youths had known little of what prison was like before their visit to Risley.

Both interviewees thought the project was a good thing and said the experience had changed their view of prison. One had been particularly horrified by the prison clothes and sheets, describing the conditions as "lousy" and both had been very shocked by the photographs of "mangled bodies" in car accidents, which had put them off driving in stolen cars. They had found the prison officers strict: one interviewee described the prison officers as being "like the inmates, quite hard"; the other had been surprised that he had had to put his cigarette out and received "a proper frisking – not like the police".

While one offender said the visit had made it generally less likely that he would commit further offences, the other said that, while it would make him think twice before getting involved in car crime, he did not think the visit would have much effect on other types of his offending behaviour.

## Discussion

A number of difficulties seem to lie behind the somewhat fitful operation and low referral rate of the scheme over the first two years of its operation. One issue that must be associated with the low referral rate is the scheme's exclusive concentration on car crime. This obviously limits the potential target group considerably – although it must be said that car crime is a common category of offence in the target group of males aged between 12 and 21. This issue was mentioned by a number of the referrers, one of whom, while preferring the less-confrontational style of the Risley scheme to the GPIES approach (which he described as "tantamount to child abuse"), thought that social services might be more interested in the Garth scheme because they would take a wider range of referrals. A youth justice team manager from another department who was briefly interviewed also thought it would be more useful if the scheme was extended to other offence categories, such as burglars and violent offenders at risk of custody. However, it should be noted that the two social workers interviewed from one of the social services departments said that they would not use the project unless it was focused exclusively on motor offending.

The offence specific nature of the CRCS also carries implications for the potential extent of any desistance. One of the young offenders said that while the scheme had discouraged him from getting involved in further car crime, he did not think it would have any impact on other types of offending behaviour.

A related issue is that the project seemed not only to concentrate on car crime – but more specifically on joy-riding: much of the material concentrated on showing the potential impact of joy-riding on victims and offenders. While the reason for this is clear in terms of the history of the scheme's development and the powerful images that can be deployed in the presentation, it has to be questioned whether the material would have great relevance for a young offender who had stolen cars for resale or to get from 'A' to 'B'.

Another factor that seems to have affected the referral rate – or at least the satisfaction of agencies using the scheme – is the degree of confrontation. A video of the scheme in its early days showed the project to have been very different before the "new approach": individuals thought to be disruptive were intimidated and on one occasion threatened with physical violence; in another instance a youth was made to sit on a pot in front of the whole group. This change in approach was largely a response to feedback from referring agencies, but it may also have been due to changes in composition of the inmate teams involved in the scheme. Although they had considerable respect for the confrontational technique adopted by the original inmates, none of the inmates currently involved in the scheme seemed to be inter- ested in adopting an aggressive role. The social services referrers seemed happy with the lower level of confrontation adopted in the new approach, but the motor project worker was more critical – in his view the scheme had "lost a bit of its bite".

Another identified problem with the CRCS was that of participants failing to turn up at the prison. Sometimes quite large groups of young offenders were expected to attend, but only one or two actually arrived at the prison gate. Obviously, the scheme is limited in what it can do to combat this problem. Many of the potential participants in these schemes are bound to be chaotic and unreliable – and will frequently fail to turn up for appointments at social services or probation offices. However, if a greater number of referrals could be attracted for each session, one or two would not be missed if they did not turn up.

An important feature of the CRCS is its two-phased approach. A recurrent criticism of encounter groups in the research literature is that they fail to provide structured follow-up services – or that any counselling that is provided tends to be given a low priority (O'Malley *et al*. 1993). It is generally accepted that these brief, prison-based sessions are unlikely to have a prolonged effect on offending unless embedded within more long- term work focused on challenging offending behaviour. While this part of the process is largely outside the hands of the inmate-run programmes, the follow-ups conducted by the CRCS offer a means of making a contri- bution. Of course, this must be easier to achieve at a category C prison like Risley than higher security establishments. Referrers and participants were generally positive about the follow-up sessions. However, it is notable that apart from these prisoner-led follow ups there was no formal follow-up process instituted by the referring agencies themselves. This raises an important issue for effectiveness: while there is general agree- ment that these schemes can only have a significant effect on reoffending if they are an integrated part of a court order or a larger project, there seems little effort on the part of referring agencies to integrate fully the visit into other work on offending behaviour.

# 5 The Maidstone Prison Youth Project

## Background

The germs of the idea of setting up a youth project at Maidstone came from an inmate's "accumulated visits" trip[1] to another prison to see his father. During the visit, this inmate, who played the guitar and had written a number of songs about religion and life in prison, spoke and sang some songs to a group of young prisoners. He was surprised by their rapt attention and the effect the music seemed to have on them. On his return to Maidstone, he tried to set up some trips to Young Offender Institutions with the purpose of playing music, but it proved impossible to get permission.

Around this time, the inmate began playing music with a prisoner in a neighbouring cell, who played keyboards, and who became interested in the original inmate's idea of trying to divert young offenders from crime through music. As it was proving impossible to organise trips outside the prison, they decided to try to get young people to come inside. However, it was another two and a half years before the first session of the Maidstone Prison Youth Project (MPYP) took place.

The first session was held in March 1993, and since then there have been two more. This project differs greatly from the other two, chiefly in its emphasis on music and the number and nature of the participating youths. The music is performed by the two founding inmates, a prison-based probation officer and two other inmates. Referrals have come mainly from youth centres, schools and young offender teams. One hundred and twenty such people attended the first session; 75 the second and 260 the third. The variation in the numbers attending seems to have reflected variation in the project's success in attracting referrals, rather than any conscious effort to vary the number of participants. The observed session was the third since the scheme had begun operation – and was filmed for a 'Panorama' documentary which was broadcast in late 1993.

While the idea of the MPYP has been developed primarily by the two founding inmates, there has been considerable support and input from other sections of the prison. The head of inmate activities, the prison

---

1    If a prisoner is located some distance from his home, he can accumulate his permitted number of visits and have them over a longer period during which he is located at a prison closer to home.

chaplain, the seconded probation team and other inmates associated with the project have played major parts in ensuring the scheme's development and survival.

## Location, target group and referral process

As with the GPIES and the first year of the CRCS's operation, the MPYP is based in the prison chapel: a purpose-built Victorian building. The reasons for this appear to be basically practical: the chapel is the only sizeable auditorium available and, being housed in a single, separate building, allows loud music to be played without disturbing other parts of the prison. However, it may also be relevant that the prison chaplain is a key supporter of the project and the originating inmate is a committed Christian, involved with religious activities in the chapel.

The target group for the project is very broad. While there has been a commitment to including at least some young offenders in the audience, the two inmates running the project thought it was important to get a mixture of convicted offenders and youths with no previous convictions. Two reasons were given for including the latter group: first, many young people without a criminal record will have been involved in offending behaviour but not been caught and second, even if they had not committed any offences, a principal aim of the project was to *deter* young people from crime.

Referrals have therefore come from ordinary schools, youth centres and the local YMCA branch, as well as from social services and the probation service. It was difficult for the inmates to keep precise records on the number and origin of referrals, due to the fact that referrers were often vague or inaccurate about the number of young people they were bringing to the project. However, records were available for 240 of the estimated 260 youths thought to have attended the observed session. Of these, only 10 per cent were from social services and therefore known offenders. Thirty-six per cent were from youth centres, the YMCA or a detached youth project; 33 per cent from "ordinary" schools and 22 per cent from special schools. It cannot be assumed that the youths from the schools and youth centres were not offenders – indeed telephone conversations with referrers revealed that some teachers and youth leaders had purposefully selected young people who had been in trouble with the police before. There were four special schools that referred young people to the project – but these seemed to differ considerably in nature. While one worked mainly with young people with learning difficulties, another was aimed at young people with a disruptive history in schools, who had been expelled or excluded from other establishments.

## Objectives

The principal aim of the scheme is to deter young people from crime by describing conditions in prison and by stressing how easy it is to end up in prison. The two inmates principally responsible for the scheme believed that many children had a romantic or glamourised image of prison and their aim was to counter such an image with an honest but hard-hitting description of life inside an adult prison. As with the other schemes, emphasis was put on the inmates' ability to empathise with the youths. The introductory leaflet entitled "It's better out than in" states that "our strongest asset is that we have been where they are now and can relate without patronising". Rock music is used as the principal method of conveying these messages on the basis that music will hold the attention of young people better than any other means.

## A description of the programme

The observed event was the third to be held and approximately 260 young people attended. The actual event was preceded a week before by an introductory, "pre-event briefing" for referrers, in which an outline of the programme was given and any queries answered.

On the day of the event itself, the groups of boys and girls arriving at the prison with their teachers/youth workers were shown into the waiting room beside the prison gate. The room soon filled up and there was a general air of excitement and expectancy. They watched the prison officers on the gate with fascination. The officers seemed to behave in their usual way – there was a lot of joking and banter between them as the shift changed. There was certainly no show of dourness put on for the visitors.

When a large enough proportion of the youths had arrived, a group of about 50 were taken to see one of the prison wings en route to the chapel. This wing was a typical, narrow, 'T' shaped Victorian wing. It was about 1.00 pm and all the inmates were locked in their cells after lunch. The youths were shown an empty cell and the slopping-out area, which smelt unpleasant. While the silent atmosphere and the spartan appearance of the wing would have shocked most people who had not been in prison before, this large group of youths was excitable and confident and did not seem overawed by their experience. This group was then taken on to the chapel and the other groups were taken through the wing. Once at the chapel, the youths were given a leaflet containing the lyrics to the songs and they then filed along the pews and sat in groups with their teachers or project workers. There appeared to be nearly as many girls as boys in the audience and most appeared to be in their early teens. The general atmosphere in the chapel was one of an open day – both the young people and inmates seemed somewhat nervous and excited.

Once the chapel was filled, the lights went down and the music started without introduction. It was loud, professional-sounding rock and the youths who a moment before had been chatting and fooling round were immediately rapt. The first song, about the pain of imprisonment and the desire for freedom was followed by applause from the audience. The founding inmate then outlined the aims of the programme to the audience. Another five songs were then performed, interspersed with talks about life in prison by the two inmates who had written the songs. A number of themes were covered in the talks between songs, including the feeling of powerlessness associated with imprisonment; how even the toughest inmates can become depressed and commit suicide; and how it took only one mistake to end up in prison. The founding inmate described how he had shot someone dead during the course of a robbery, making the point that he had lost his head once and wrecked his life. During the music and talk, a video or slides were shown on a large screen above the band. The images consisted of a mixture of stark pictures of prisons and prison life and pictures of victims of violent crime.

It was interesting that the young people's attention remained fixed on the singers during the talks between songs. This brought to mind the reverence given to pop stars when they speak between songs at live performances. However, on the negative side, while many of the song lyrics were very powerful, it was impossible to read them in the leaflets once the lights were turned down. A number of youths made an obvious effort to read them but had to give up.

After the first six songs a presentation was given by a local community police officer. The audience became restless and noisy – partly, no doubt, due to having been seated on uncomfortable pews for half an hour but also because of an obvious and seemingly universal dislike of the police amongst the audience. As the talk continued, the audience became more disruptive. At one stage the founding inmate came off the stage and walked into the crowd, seating himself amongst a particularly unruly group of boys. They stopped fooling around immediately. After the police presentation, two prison officers gave a presentation on the prison segregation unit and showed the audience a body belt, a strait-jacket and the coarse blanket prisoners are given to sleep under. The audience paid more attention.

There followed eight more songs, after which there was a brief tea break, followed by group discussions. During the second session of music the audience seemed to be less attentive and at one point one of the inmates stopped the music and shouted at them to keep quiet. This proved effective. The tea break was very chaotic, as 260 young people crowded around two tables trying to get a cup of tea. The group discussion was also similarly disorganised, as the participants were not properly assigned to particular groups – they just went to the nearest one. Teachers and youth workers were asked to go into one of the rooms behind the main auditorium, so that the young people and inmates could have a frank discussion. An inmate led the discussion in each group, answering any questions the youths had and talking about some of the issues raised by the songs and presentations. It was noticeable that a small number of youths remained in their pews and did not attend any of the groups.

After the group sessions, the youths left the chapel. Outside there were four or five prison officers with Alsatians lining the route to the prison gate. This had been set up as part of the programme. On reaching the prison gate, both the inner and outer gates were opened simultaneously to allow the young people to leave (they are usually only opened one at a time because of the security risk).

A week after the event a "post-event feedback" session was held, to which all referrers were invited. A number of important issues were raised at the feed-back session. There was a general consensus that the event had been rather chaotic and it was suggested that the organisers should limit the number of people attending. It was decided that the maximum number would be 150 in future sessions. Another issue raised was the fact that youths could not read the lyrics on the sheets provided because of the low lighting. It was suggested that lyric sheets be made available before the event, to allow people to familiarise themselves with the messages of the songs before they attend the event. The organisers thought this was a good idea – and planned to make the leaflets available for the next session. Another suggestion was that youths from the same parties should be divided up for the discussion groups – and perhaps when they arrived in the chapel. It was decided that youths would be given a numbered disk on arrival to denote which discus-sion group they had to attend. At the conclusion of the feedback session, the inmates asked whether they thought the scheme was worthwhile and should continue – there was a resounding positive response.

## Views of referrers

### Agencies and types of referrals

Face-to-face interviews were carried out with a teacher from a special school that had referred 12 pupils to the MPYP and with a teacher from a boys grammar school that had referred between 20 and 25 boys to the project.[2] Conversations were also held with referrers that were met at the event and the feedback session. The special school was contacted at random from a list of referrers and it was not until the researcher arrived to conduct the inter-

---

2    It was only possible to interview a small sample of the large pool of referrers who sent pupils to the MPYP. The rather critical views expressed by the grammer school teacher do not appear to have been representative of the school teachers as a whole. According to project staff, he was the only teacher who did not use the project again on future occasions.

views that he realised that it was a school for young people with severe learning difficulties. This made it difficult to carry out participant interviews, although with the help of staff at the school, some discussions were carried out with the young people. The 12 students that the staff had referred were aged between 16 and 19 and had been selected as the more able of the students attending the school. Their teacher said that few of her students were ever likely to get in to trouble – they were "too dependent and child-like". However, she thought that one of the students who had attended "thought he was very street-wise" and was on the verges of petty crime. He had been to court to give evidence when a friend of his was prosecuted, but had not been charged himself. However, the teacher interviewed was using the MPYP as a component in a "citizenship" course, rather than as a crime prevention project. As part of this course, the students were taken to a range of public institutions, including a museum, a doctor's surgery, a police station and a court.

The teacher at the boys grammar school had asked for volunteers, rather than selecting boys for the visit. Nevertheless, he thought that there were four or five amongst the group who were probably on the fringes of crime and he had made a special effort to get them interested in the visit. All the boys who attended were aged between 15 and 16.

## Overall impressions

The special school teacher was generally impressed by the scheme, although she thought there had been far too many children there. The referral system had been efficient and the inmates and prison officers had performed their roles well. However, for her purposes, a simple tour around the prison would have sufficed.

The grammar school teacher was fairly critical of the scheme. While he thought the scheme was potentially useful as a general, educative project for ordinary pupils, he did not think it would have any impact on hardened young offenders. He thought the "hard nuts" would have ignored the messages. Moreover, the session he attended had been very disorganised: there were far too many children and because they were mostly disruptive, rowdy pupils, they were very hard to control. This had two detrimental effects: first, many of the messages of the project were lost amongst the background noise and distraction and second, the prison officers had been "obsessed" with security, which had resulted in their group being herded through the wings much too fast. He was also unhappy about the way teachers had to relinquish control of their pupils to the inmates: there had been a lot of chaos with children roaming around and not attending the group sessions. Moreover, he did not trust the inmates entirely: he had been unsettled by a pupil's report that an inmate had told one of the groups of children that a prisoner had been kicked to death by prison officers inside Maidstone. He did not think such protests should be made by the inmates: there was not enough recognition of the fact that many of these prisoners were serving sentences for serious offences.

## Level of confrontation

This was a less significant feature for the MPYP, in that the inmates were considerably less confrontational than the other two schemes and the small amount of aggression that was displayed was all "on stage", and therefore some distance from the children and not individually targeted as in other schemes. The special school teacher thought the mix of confrontation and education had been "about right": her pupils had been more intimidated by the other children than the inmates. The grammar school teacher had not found the confrontational parts very convincing: one of the inmates swore a lot, but he thought his pupils had seen through this "attempt at street cred". He had found the project a lot less hard-edged than the publicity material had suggested.

## Criticisms

Apart from the issue of overcrowding, the only other criticism the special school teacher had was that the police officer had not come over very well. The grammar school teacher was also critical of the police presentation: "he came across as the stereotypical PC plod and was a sitting duck with all those children there". He had also found the prison officer talk "morbid, out of context and unsupported." He had been quite shocked that one of the inmates had related how he had shot a bank manager three times in the head. He did not think this was at all necessary. Finally, he thought a lot of the music was old-fashioned and out of touch – "70's rock...these kids aren't in to Led Zeppelin."

## Follow-up

The special school teacher thought that the follow-up was "all-important". She had talked with her group about their visit, and each of the students had written up a piece on how they felt about their experience. The teacher from the grammar school had not followed up the visit to the MPYP, because he had not thought it was any good. They had only sent the children because the scheme had been desperate to make up numbers, and would not use the scheme again.

### *Effectiveness*

All the pupils from the special school had known about prison before their visit to the MPYP had been gleaned from television. The teacher thought that it had probably been quite a shock for them to learn that places like HMP Maidstone existed. There was a tendency for the general public to view prisons as a holiday camp – and the scheme could be very useful for showing schoolchildren what the reality of prison-life was like. The grammar school teacher was obviously very critical of the session he had attended, but was unsure what impact the scheme may have had on his pupils. He thought the disorganisation and peer-group banter had probably protected them from having to think about the issues. More generally, he thought that such projects could be useful in so far as there was a disparity between young peoples' images of prison and reality. He too referred to the holiday camp image of imprisonment that was conveyed by the media. It was probably a good idea to show children that conditions in prison were shocking, but he thought this would be very hard to set up due to what he perceived as "the stranglehold" on school time created by the national curriculum. It was very difficult to justify broader "citizenship" education within this narrow definition of education.

## Views of participants

A brief discussion was held with a group of six of the participants from the special school. None of them had been in prison or had relatives who had been in prison. All that they had known about prison they had learnt from television. A number of the students had been saddened by their visit: they had not liked the interiors of the cells or the handcuffs and strait-jackets. They had liked the music, although they found it a bit loud and had not understood the words. They had found the slides and videos disquieting: prison was a bad place to be, and they felt sorry for the prisoners.

Four of the grammar school boys who had attended the MPYP were interviewed in a group. They were all 16-years-old and had volunteered to attend, because they had been interested to get "an inside view" of prison. While none of them admitted to having been in trouble before, they said that some of the other boys that had attended were "heading for trouble". They had known very little about prisons before their visit – only what they had seen on the television.

They all thought the project was worthwhile: "it made you think". They thought the group sessions with the inmates had been the best part – although the groups were a little too large and they had found it difficult to ask questions with so many strangers present. They had also been struck by the visit to the wing and the guards with Alsatians. One of the boys said "It was a much more depressing place than I'd thought it would be – it really hit you."

They had found the music too loud and some of the songs hard to understand. They could remember one song about an inmate killing himself – and that the general theme of many of the songs was how depressing life in prison was. The singing went on for too long and the boys felt that the inmates were quite repetitive. However, they had been impressed by the slides and videos.

With regard to changing the scheme for the better, the consensus was that there should be less music and more time in groups. They had asked questions about life inside during the groups – and the inmates had been very informative. They thought it was good for the teachers to be sent elsewhere for the young people to be able to talk with the inmates on their own. All four thought the project had had a "big effect" on them: "you never want to be sent there... it's definitely made me less likely to offend."

## Discussion

Before reaching any conclusions about the Maidstone scheme, two points should be stressed. First, the project is still at an early stage of development and there is every indication from the observation of the feedback session that the organisers are learning from their mistakes. Second, according to referrers and inmates, the observed session was the most disorganised and ineffective of the three so far carried out, chiefly due to the very large number of youths who attended. This was the session that the referrer and participant interviewees had attended.

An interesting feature of the MPYP is its very broad target group, including school children who are not suspected of being involved in crime. If the scheme was more confrontational this would be problematic, as it would be particularly unethical to intimidate children who had not even countenanced the idea of committing crime. However, the approach of the MPYP is broadly educational rather than confrontational, the aim being to inform young people about what prison life is like and thereby, it is hoped, to deter them from crime. It should also be noted here that an educational approach aimed at school children could have an effect beyond the potential offending behaviour of the individuals attending the project. If young people went away with a powerful image of the dangerous, depressing and destructive nature of imprisonment, it is possible that they could have some influence on the behaviour of friends, partners and siblings. Interesting in this respect was the reaction of a girl in one of the observed discussion groups, who asked the inmate about his family and was obviously moved by his account of a recent "Dear John" letter, and the loss of contact with his children. While schoolgirls are a low risk group with regard to their own offending behaviour, there is still the possibility of a vicarious preventative effect.

Against such arguments is the possibility that both non-offenders and offenders could, through a process of "hero-worship", end up identifying with the prisoners and the criminal behaviour that landed them in prison. This argument has particular force in the context of the MPYP, where the prisoners take on something of the personae of pop stars, and might thereby be particularly attractive role models. Evidence that this might have been happening came from a telephone conversation with a referrer to the scheme who said that a young person he had taken to the project had asked an inmate for his autograph. However, the grammar school teacher who was interviewed did not think that this issue was a problem, due to the very clear negative message about life inside delivered by the inmates. It could be that the younger, more vulnerable children are more likely to idolise the inmates than the others.

The other two projects seem to have gone through problematic phases when the originating inmates have left the prison and other inmates have had to take over. Maidstone is unlikely to be an exception to this rule: at the time of writing, one of the two founding inmates is now living in the prison hostel and the other is overdue for a transfer to another establishment. While there was some tendency for the inmates involved in all the projects to see themselves as irreplaceable, this has particular validity in the case of the MPYP. According to the inmates involved they have to be "doing it for the right reasons" i.e., unselfish motivation, but they must also be musically talented. It is apparently proving difficult to locate such people within a single prison like Maidstone.

Finally, a practical problem for the MPYP which needs to be overcome is the lack of adequate access to a telephone. This issue is especially significant given the very large groups of youths attending. At present many of the referrals are taken by the Prison Chaplain on the telephone line in his office attached to the chapel, but this was proving a heavy administrative burden. One of the inmates associated with the scheme had permission to use the phone in the Chaplain's presence, but this was virtually useless, as the scheme needed someone to answer the telephone when the Chaplain was absent. A possible future answer to the problem suggested by the Chaplain was to bring a volunteer in to the prison to handle the referrals.

# 6 Conclusions

A clear conclusion of the research conducted so far is that the schemes under study represent three very different approaches to youth crime prevention. In summary, while the GPIES is a fairly confrontational scheme aimed at a wide range of young offenders, the CRCS is a broadly educational project aimed only at motor offenders and the MPYP is an educational project aimed at virtually any young person. The critical factors distinguishing between the projects are therefore the size and nature of their target groups and the degree of confrontation employed. These features are connected in that it seems ethically unacceptable for a highly confrontational project to be directed at unconvicted school children, but the more educational a project, the more acceptable it would be for a broad range of young people to attend. The three projects seem to fit this rule to some extent, in that the least confrontational project, the MPYP, has the broadest target group. Interestingly, both the CRCS and the GPIES have shown a tendency to diversify away from probation and social service referrals over the course of their operation. In the case of the more confrontational GPIES this seems an unfortunate development.

This said, it should be stressed that there are many very vulnerable and emotionally unstable young people who commit offences: just because they are "young offenders" does not mean that they can cope with a highly emotionally charged and personally confrontational programme. It is therefore important that referrers carefully assess offenders before sending them to a confrontational project like the GPIES. While all interviewed referrers using the GPIES and CRCS had excluded potential referrals on the basis of emotional vulnerability, there seemed to be considerable variation among referrers in the extent of assessment and the proportion screened out. A further important safeguard is the provision of detailed information on the young people attending the schemes, a process which the GPIES seemed to manage very effectively. More important still is the issue of whether confrontational schemes should be used at the pre-sentence stage. If offenders are given custodial sentences immediately after attending the GPIES or CRCS, the highly negative portrayal of prison life could increase any feelings of desperation and contribute to the risk of suicide. Both these schemes take young people at the pre-sentence stage.

As well as the potential damage to more vulnerable young people, there are other reasons for keeping the confrontational content of presentations to a minimum. Highly confrontational approaches are likely to lead to the closure of schemes. The Australian 'Day in Prison' programme described by O'Malley *et al.* (1993) was temporarily suspended after allegations that youths were assaulted by prison officers. In this country, an investigation of a day visit programme at Eversthorpe was launched after allegations that among other things, youths were made to sit on a piss-pot and go through the motions of wiping their bottoms with toilet paper in front of the whole group. Perhaps unsurprisingly, the investigation by the social services found the programme to be abusive. It is interesting that these two recent examples of alleged abuse took place in countries other than the US: it appears that the UK and Australia may have failed to profit from the lessons learned from America's much longer experimentation with day visits. Lastly, there is an inevitable tendency for very confrontational schemes to exaggerate the violence and degradation of prison life. This is unnecessary: as some interviewees pointed out, life in most British prisons is sufficiently unpleasant to put anyone off spending any time inside them – there is no need for fiction. A minimum of theatrics and a maximum of honesty would seem to be the best approach to presentations. A number of young people who were interviewed were very suspicious that inmates were, in their own words, "bullshitting" them – in one case some youths had come away with the impression that the inmates were professional actors.

An interesting feature of the CRCS is its concentration on car crime. While the reason for this focus can be traced to the early development of the scheme, there is an indication that it may have led to a low and unreliable referral rate. While car crime is undoubtably a common offence in the target age group, there is the problem that only a proportion of potential referrers are likely to use any prison-based encounter group. Many social workers and probation officers are likely to be opposed to the idea of any project which sounds confrontational or punishing. In this light, the CRCS's move away from a confrontational approach in reaction to feedback from referring agencies seems significant.

One of the most outstanding features of the discussions held with prisoners was their great enthusiasm and commitment to the three projects. Prisoners at each prison seemed genuine in their desire to divert young people from crime and imprisonment and were very positive about their work on the projects. On the subject of motivation, many inmates stressed that they would not stand to gain personally from their involvement. However, some probation staff and referrers suggested that this was not entirely true: working on the project was likely to give them a trusted status, allowing them more freedom to move around the prison and giving them a better prospect for home leave, and their involvement could certainly do no harm to their prospects for early release. On a less selfish note, two of the worst aspects of prison life according to prisoners are boredom and isolation. Involvement in the projects provided a comparatively worthwhile and interesting way to pass their time, and a means to meet people from outside the prison – both youths and referrers. The only real problem with regard to prisoner motivation seemed to be the possibility of over-involvement. One interviewee referred to the danger that lifers in particular could become quite dependent on the schemes, as a source of interest and self-worth. The fact that some of these prisoners put a lot of effort and emotion into the project can also lead to an unrealistic expectation of something in return, and bitter disappointment when hopes are dashed. In conclusion, it is important to stress that a lifer's involvement in one of these projects is not akin to the involvement of a member of the public in a similar scheme outside prison. Their participation can become a rather important part of their lives, for which they are quite prepared to turn down a move to a lower security prison.

The involvement of lifers raises a number of other issues. In the context of the GPIES, can an adolescent cautioned for vandalism relate his position to that of a contract killer serving life? There is the danger that young offenders will dismiss the advice given to them on the grounds that they would never murder someone and thereby end up serving a life sentence at Garth. On the other hand, lifers tend to be able to work on such projects for a long period of time, are generally trusted by prison staff and may also contribute to the acceptance of the project amongst other inmates, on account of their prestigious status. It should also be noted that lifers are the driving force behind two of the schemes.

A very important issue that deserves further attention is the follow-up to the prison visit. It is generally accepted that the prison visits are unlikely to have any demonstrable effect on offending behaviour unless they are an integral part of a larger package of measures designed to prevent offending. Yet there was little evidence of a close integration of the programme within court orders or other activities. The project often seemed to provide a stand-alone "component" of a court order. The CRCS is the only scheme to provide regular follow-ups by inmates – but this is partly because the inmates involved are all category C security and it is therefore, presumably, easier to allow them outside the prison. While other schemes might be able to arrange follow-up sessions inside the prison, it has been pointed out by referrers and inmates at the CRCS that the value in their follow-ups is that the young offenders are on their own territory and are much more confident about asking questions. However, the main responsibility for ensuring that day visits are part of an effective package must lie with the supervising probation officers, social workers, youth leaders and teachers. It was surprising that none of the referrers conducted one-to-one follow-up sessions with participants as standard practice. While some organised groups sessions, male adolescents are notoriously reluctant to speak frankly about their experiences and feelings in such groups.

An important conclusion that has come out of this study of three widely differing schemes is that there is scope for tailoring programmes to particular target groups: providing variety both across prisons and within individual prisons, which could vary their presentation according to the group attending. The needs of children with learning difficulties on a citizenship course will be different from those of recidivist young offenders on the brink of a custodial sentence.

The potential for purely educational programmes seems very great: referrers and participants frequently pointed out that all young people knew of prison was what they learned from the media – and much of this "information" only served to glamourise prisoners and criminals – or describe prisons as holiday camps. Participant interviews also revealed that, even if close relatives had served prison sentences, there was often very little discussion of what the experience had been like. There may therefore be a strong case for setting up prison-based programmes which show school children the reality of life inside British prisons.

With regard to programmes for young offenders, again there seems to be a need for diversity. One of the referrers was using two different prison schemes for young offenders: a broadly educational scheme at HMP Nottingham for those at the start of their criminal careers and the GPIES for those at high risk of custody.

## Key issues for setting up projects

In setting up new schemes, a number of recommendations can be made on the basis of this research.

- The selection of the target group will have great implications for the nature of the project – confrontational approaches should be restricted to cautioned or convicted offenders.

- No offenders should be referred to projects at the pre-sentence stage. The highly negative and threatening portrayal of prison life presented by these projects could lead to self-injury and suicide if offenders receive prison sentences having visited the projects.

- Formal assessment procedures should be put in place – particularly for more confrontational schemes. Sensitive and vulnerable young people should be filtered out.

- Confrontation should be minimised wherever possible: a minimum of theatrics and a maximum of honesty would seem to be the best approach.

- While projects seem to be very effectively set up and run by inmates, Governors should keep a close eye on their development and sessions must always be observed by prison staff. Projects should also always be observed by referrers – either *in situ* or on video.

- It is important for referrers to provide inmates in advance with as much information as possible about the young people attending, so that inmates can tailor the presentation to the audience/participants.

- Preparation and follow-up are likely to be critical to any effect of the scheme. Projects for offenders should form an integral part of larger packages of measures designed to prevent offending. It is also important that young offenders get a chance to speak about their visit with their probation officer or social worker on their own, as a formal follow-up procedure.

- There are pros and cons to the involvement of long-term prisoners and lifers with these projects. On the one hand, adolescents with little criminal involvement might reject the advice offered because they cannot envisage themselves ever committing very serious crimes and serving long prison sentences. On the other hand, lifers provide continuity, being able to work on projects for long periods of time before being moved, are generally trusted by prison staff and may also contribute to the acceptance of the project amongst other inmates, on account of their prestigious status. They may also have the time and motivation to get schemes running in the first place.

- There is a potential for over-commitment on the part of inmates working on these schemes, which argues for quite careful supervision of the individual inmates involved – perhaps by seconded probation officers or prison psychologists.

- The main forces behind the development of all the case study projects were highly-motivated and charismatic inmates. There was a tendency for projects to go through a crisis when the founding inmates were moved on. Schemes may need considerable support at this stage – with careful selection and "training" of replacement inmates.

- While access to telephones is a problematic issue in prisons, it is imperative that someone associated with the project has access to a telephone to receive referrals. If inmates cannot be allowed such access, it might be possible to have volunteers come in to prisons to handle referrals.

- Projects should build-in the opportunity for feedback from referrers on a regular basis, to inform their development.

In conclusion, day visits to prison have moved on a long way from the Rahway "scared straight" model. Even in this country, where the idea is comparatively new, there is already a diverse range of schemes in operation. The original, highly confrontational model can be seen as one end of a continuum that runs through to purely educational approaches. Perhaps the most exciting potential for future development is the idea of developing schemes to inform school children about imprisonment – both as part of their general education and as a means of crime prevention. While this might profit society in general, it should not be forgotten that these schemes are also of great benefit to the inmates involved and, perhaps, more generally, to the prison regimes. As a Governor of one of the prisons pointed out, prisons are essentially negative institutions: they lock up wrong-doers – it is very refreshing for inmates to be involved in trying to do something positive.

# References

**Berg, B.L.** (1986). *'Inmate Participation in a Delinquency Deterrence Programme, The Youth Assistance Program – Florida'*. Paper presented at the 38th Annual Meeting of the American Society of Criminology. Atlanta, Georgia.

**Brodsky, S.L.** (1970). 'The Prisoner as Agent of Attitude Change: A Study of Prison Profile Effects.' *British Journal of Criminology*, 10, 280-285.

**Buckner, J.C. and Chesney-Lind, M.** (1983). 'Dramatic Cures for Juvenile Crime: An Evaluation of a Prisoner-run Delinquency Prevention Programme.' *Criminal Justice and Behaviour*, 10, 2, 227-247.

**Corrigan, J.W.** (1979). 'Scared Straight! Controversy Surrounds Inmate Program.' *Youth Forum*, 3, 6.

**Finckenauer, J.O.** (1978). *Juvenile Awareness Project Evaluation, report no.1.* New Brunswick, New Jersey: Rutgers University School of Criminal Justice.

**Finckenauer, J.O.** (1979). *Juvenile Awareness Project Evaluation, report no.2.* New Brunswick, New Jersey: Rutgers University School of Criminal Justice.

**Finckenauer, J.O.** (1982). *Scared Straight! and the Panacea Phenomenon.* New Jersey: Prentice-Hall.

**Homant, R.J. and Osowski, G.** (1981). 'Evaluation of the "Scared Straight" Model: Some Methodological and Political Consideration.' *Corrective and Social Psychiatry and Journal of Behaviour Technology Methods and Therapy*, 27, 3, 130-134.

**Keller, R.L.** (1986). *Some latent effects of a delinquency prevention programme on adult inmate-counsellors at the Colorado State Penitentiary.* Paper presented at the 38th Annual Meeting of the American Society of Criminology. Atlanta, Georgia.

**Langer, A.** (1979). *The Rahway State Prison Lifer's Group: A Critical Analysis.* Union, New Jersey: Kean College Department of Sociology and Social Work.

**Lewis, R.V.** (1983). 'Scared Straight California Style: Evaluation of the San Quentin Squires Programme.' *Criminal Justice and Behaviour,* 10, 2, 209-226.

**Logan, W.** (1989). 'Description of "Scared Straight" Programmes'. In National Institute of Justice: Shock Incarceration: *An Overview of Existing Programmes,* Appendix A.

**O'Malley, P., Coventry, G. and Walters, R.** (1993). Victoria's "Day in Prison Program": an evaluation and critique. *Australian and New Zealand Journal of Criminology,* 26, 171-183.22.

# Publications

## List of Research and Planning Unit Publications

The Research and Planning Unit (previously the Research Unit) has been publishing its work since 1955, and a list of reports for the last three years is provided below. A **full** list of publications is available on request from the Research and Planning Unit.

## Home Office Research Studies (HORS)

125. **Magistrates' court or Crown Court? Mode of trial decisions and sentencing.** Carol Hedderman and David Moxon. 1992. vii + 53pp. (0 11 341036 0).

126. **Developments in the use of compensation orders in magistrates' courts since October 1988.** David Moxon, John Martin Corkery and Carol Hedderman. 1992. x + 48pp. (0 11 341042 5).

127. **A comparative study of firefighting arrangements in Britain, Denmark, the Netherlands and Sweden.** John Graham, Simon Field, Roger Tarling and Heather Wilkinson. 1992. x + 57pp. (0 11 341043 3).

128. **The National Prison Survey 1991: main findings.** Roy Walmsley, Liz Howard and Sheila White. 1992. xiv + 82pp. (0 11 341051 4).

129. **Changing the Code: police detention under the revised PACE Codes of Practice.** David Brown, Tom Ellis and Karen Larcombe. 1992. viii + 122pp. (0 11 341052 2).

130. **Car theft: the offender's perspective.** Roy Light, Claire Nee and Helen Ingham. 1993. x + 89pp. (0 11 341069 7).

131. **Housing, Community and Crime: The Impact of the Priority Estates Project.** Janet Foster and Timothy Hope with assistance from Lizanne Dowds and Mike Sutton. 1993. xi + 118pp. (0 11 341078 6).

132. **The 1992 British Crime Survey.** Pat Mayhew, Natalie Aye Maung and Catriona Mirrlees-Black. 1993. xiii + 206pp. ( 0 11 341094 8).

133. **Intensive Probation in England and Wales: an evaluation.** George Mair, Charles Lloyd, Claire Nee and Rae Sibbett. 1994. xiv + 143pp. ( 0 11 341114 6).

134. **Contacts between Police and Public: findings from the 1992 British Crime Survey.** Wesley G Skogan. 1995. ix + 93pp. (0 11 341115 4).

135. **Policing low-level disorder : Police use of Section 5 of the Public Order Act 1986.** David Brown and Tom Ellis. 1994. ix + 69pp. (0 11 341116 2).

136. **Explaining reconviction rates: A critical analysis.** Charles Lloyd, George Mair and Mike Hough. 1995. xiv + 103pp. (0 11 341117 0).

137. **Case Screening by the Crown Prosecution Service: How and why cases are terminated.** Debbie Crisp and David Moxon. 1995. viii + 66pp. (0 11 341137 5).

138. **Public Interest Case Assessment Schemes.** Debbie Crisp, Claire Whittaker and Jessica Harris. 1995. x + 58pp. (0 11 341139 1).

139. **Policing domestic violence in the 1990s.** Sharon Grace. 1995. x + 74pp. (0 11 341140 5).

140. **Young people, victimisation and the police: British Crime Survey findings on experiences and attitudes of 12 to 15 year olds.** Natalie Aye Maung. 1995. xii + 140pp.

141. **The Settlement of refugees in Britain.** Jenny Carey-Wood, Karen Duke, Valerie Karn and Tony Marshall. 1995. xii + 133pp. (0 11 341145 6).

142. **Vietnamese Refugees since 1982.** Karen Duke and Tony Marshall. 1995. x + 62pp. (0 11 341147 2).

143. **The Parish Special Constables Scheme.** Peter Southgate, Tom Bucke and Carole Byron. 1995. x + 59pp. (1 85893 458 3).

144. **Measuring the Satisfaction of the Courts with the Probation Service.** Chris May. 1995. x + 76pp. (1 85893 483 4).

# Research and Planning Unit Papers (RPUP)

65. **Offending while on bail: a survey of recent studies.** Patricia M. Morgan. 1992.

66. **Juveniles sentenced for serious offences: a comparison of regimes in Young Offender Institutions and Local Authority Community Homes.** John Ditchfield and Liza Catan. 1992.

67. **The management and deployment of police armed response vehicles.** Peter Southgate. 1992.

68. **Using psychometric personality tests in the selection of firearms officers.** Catriona Mirrlees-Black. 1992.

69. **Bail information schemes: practice and effect.** Charles Lloyd. 1992.

70. **Crack and cocaine in England and Wales.** Joy Mott (editor). 1992.

71. **Rape: from recording to conviction.** Sharon Grace, Charles Lloyd and Lorna J. F. Smith. 1992.

72. **The National Probation Survey 1990.** Chris May. 1993.

73. **Public satisfaction with police services.** Peter Southgate and Debbie Crisp. 1993.

74. **Disqualification from driving: an effective penalty?** Catriona Mirrlees-Black. 1993.

75. **Detention under the Prevention of Terrorism (Temporary Provisions) Act 1989: Access to legal advice and outside contact.** David Brown. 1993.

76. **Panel assessment schemes for mentally disordered offenders.** Carol Hedderman. 1993.

77. **Cash-limiting the probation service: a case study in resource allocation.** Simon Field and Mike Hough. 1993.

78. **The probation response to drug misuse.** Claire Nee and Rae Sibbitt. 1993.

79    **Approval of rifle and target shooting clubs: the effects of the new and revised criteria.** John Martin Corkery. 1993.

80.   **The long-term needs of victims: A review of the literature.** Tim Newburn. 1993.

81.   **The welfare needs of unconvicted prisoners.** Diane Caddle and Sheila White. 1994.

82.   **Racially motivated crime: a British Crime Survey analysis.** Natalie Aye Maung and Catriona Mirrlees-Black. 1994.

83.   **Mathematical models for forecasting Passport demand.** Andy Jones and John MacLeod. 1994.

84.   **The theft of firearms.** John Corkery. 1994.

85.   **Equal opportunities and the Fire Service.** Tom Bucke. 1994.

86.   **Drug Education Amongst Teenagers: a 1992 British Crime Survey Analysis.** Lizanne Dowds and Judith Redfern. 1995.

87.   **Group 4 Prisoner Escort Service: a survey of customer satisfaction.** Claire Nee. 1994.

88.   **Special Considerations: Issues for the Management and Organisation of the Volunteer Police.** Catriona Mirrlees-Black and Carole Byron. 1995.

89.   **Self-reported drug misuse in England and Wales: findings from the 1992 British Crime Survey.** Joy Mott and Catriona Mirrlees-Black. 1995.

90.   **Improving bail decisions: the bail process project, phase 1.** John Burrows, Paul Henderson and Patricia Morgan. 1995.

91.   **Practitioners' views of the Criminal Justice Act: a survey of criminal justice agencies.** George Mair and Chris May. 1995.

92.   **Obscene, threatening and other troublesome telephone calls to women in England and Wales: 1982-1992.** Wendy Buck, Michael Chatterton and Ken Pease. 1995.

93.   **A survey of the prisoner escort and custody service provided by Group 4 and by Securicor Custodial Services.** Diane Caddle. 1995.

# Research Findings

1. **Magistrates' court or Crown Court? Mode of trial decisions and their impact on sentencing.** Carol Hedderman and David Moxon. 1992.

2. **Surveying crime: findings from the 1992 British Crime Survey.** Pat Mayhew and Natalie Aye Maung. 1992.

3. **Car Theft: the offenders' perspective.** Claire Nee. 1993.

4. **The National Prison Survey 1991: main findings.** Roy Walmsley, Liz Howard and Sheila White. 1993.

5. **Changing the Code: Police detention under the revised PACE codes of practice.** David Brown, Tom Ellis and Karen Larcombe. 1993.

6. **Rifle and pistol target shooting clubs: The effects of new approval criteria.** John M. Corkery. 1993.

7. **Self-reported drug misuse in England and Wales. Main findings from the 1992 British Crime Survey.** Joy Mott and Catriona Mirrlees-Black. 1993.

8. **Findings from the International Crime Survey.** Pat Mayhew. 1994.

9 **Fear of Crime: Findings from the 1992 British Crime Survey.** Catriona Mirrlees-Black and Natalie Aye Maung. 1994.

10. **Does the Criminal Justice system treat men and women differently?** Carol Hedderman and Mike Hough. 1994.

11. **Participation in Neighbourhood Watch: Findings from the 1992 British Crime Survey.** Lizanne Dowds and Pat Mayhew. 1994.

12. **Explaining Reconviction Rates: A Critical Analysis.** Charles Lloyd, George Mair and Mike Hough. 1995.

13. **Equal opportunities and the Fire Service.** Tom Bucke. 1994.

14. **Trends in Crime: Findings from the 1994 British Crime Survey.** Pat Mayhew, Catriona Mirrlees-Black and Natalie Aye Maung. 1994.

15. **Intensive Probation in England and Wales: an evaluation.** George Mair, Charles Lloyd, Claire Nee and Rae Sibbett. 1995.

16. **The settlement of refugees in Britain.** Jenny Carey-Wood, Karen Duke, Valerie Karn and Tony Marshall. 1995.

17. **Young people, victimisation and the police: British Crime Survey findings on experiences and attitudes of 12 to 15 year olds.** Natalie Aye Maung. 1995.

18. **Vietnamese Refugees since 1982.** Karen Duke and Tony Marshall. 1995.

19. **Supervision of Restricted Patients in the Community.** Dell and Grounds. 1995.

20. **Videotaping children's evidence: an evaluation.** Graham Davies, Clare Wilson, Rebecca Mitchell and John Milsom. 1995.

## Research Bulletin

The Research Bulletin is published twice each year and contains short articles on recent research. Research Bulletin No. 37 was published recently.

## Occasional Papers

**Coping with a crisis: the introduction of three and two in a cell.** T. G. Weiler. 1992.

**Psychiatric Assessment at the Magistrates' Court.** Philip Joseph. 1992.

**Measurement of caseload weightings in magistrates' courts.** Richard J. Gadsden and Graham J. Worsdale. 1992.

**The CDE of scheduling in magistrates' courts.** John W. Raine and Michael J. Willson. 1992.

**Employment opportunities for offenders.** David Downes. 1993.

**Sex offenders: a framework for the evaluation of community-based treatment.** Mary Barker and Rod Morgan. 1993.

**Suicide attempts and self-injury in male prisons.** Alison Liebling and Helen Krarup. 1993.

**Measurement of caseload weightings associated with the Children Act.** Richard J. Gadsden and Graham J. Worsdale. 1994. (Available from the RPU Information Section.)

**Managing difficult prisoners: The Lincoln and Hull special units.** Professor Keith Bottomley, Professor Norman Jepson, Mr Kenneth Elliott and Dr Jeremy Coid. 1994. (Available from RPU Information Section.)

**The Nacro diversion intiative for mentally disturbed offenders: an account and an evaluation.** Home Office, NACRO and Mental Health Foundation. 1994. (Available from RPU Information Section.)

**Probation Motor Projects in England and Wales.** J P Martin and Douglas Martin. 1994.

**Community-based treatment of sex offenders: an evaluation of seven treatment programmes.** R Beckett, A Beech, D Fisher and A S Fordham. 1994.

**Videotaping children's evidence: an evaluation.** Graham Davies, Clare Wilson, Rebecca Mitchell and John Milsom. 1995.

**Managing the needs of female prisoners.** Allison Morris, Chris Wilkinson, Andrea Tisi, Jane Woodrow and Ann Rockley. 1995.

## Books

**Analysing Offending. Data, Models and Interpretations.** Roger Tarling. 1993. viii + 203pp. (0 11 341080 8).

## Requests for Publications

*Home Office Research Studies* from 143 onwards, *Research and Planning Unit Papers, Research Findings, the Research and Planning Unit Programme and Research Bulletins* are available on request from the Information Section, Home Office Research and Planning Unit, Room 278, 50 Queen Anne's Gate, London SW1H 9AT. Telephone: 0171 273 2084 (answering machine).

*Occasional Papers* can be purchased from: Home Office, Publications Unit, 50 Queen Anne's Gate, London SW1 9AT. Telephone: 0171 273 2302.

*Home Office Research Studies* prior to 143 can be purchased from:

**HMSO Publications Centre**
(Mail, fax and telephone orders only)
PO Box 276, London SW8 5DT
Telephone orders: 0171-873 9090
General enquiries: 0171-873 0011
(queuing system in operation for both numbers)
Fax orders: 0171-873 8200

*And also from **HMSO Bookshops***